INDIA
AND FREEDOM

INDIA
AND FREEDOM

LEOPOLD STENNETT AMERY

GYAN

Published by

Gyan Publishing House
5, Ansari Road
Daryaganj, New Delhi-110002
Phone: 011-47034999, 9811692060
E-mail: books@gyanbooks.com

Distribution Network
gyanbooks.com
India, USA, Canada, UK, Australia

ISBN: 978-93-7225-511-9 (PB)

First Published, 1942

2nd Impression 2025

Printed at: Gyan Press, Delhi.

INDIA AND FREEDOM
Author: LEOPOLD STENNETT AMERY

INDIA AND FREEDOM

INDIA
AND FREEDOM

By the Rt. Hon.
L. S. AMERY, M.P.
Secretary of State for India and Burma

1942

FOREWORD

THERE is no charge to which British public opinion has been more sensitive than the reproach that our policy towards India bears no relation to our professed war aims. We are charged with professing to fight for freedom and democracy in Europe, while denying both to India. We are charged with denouncing the spirit of new aggression and domination on the part of Germany and Japan while stubbornly resolved not to part with the fruit of old aggression in the shape of our present domination over India.

That is one charge. There is another charge, even more wounding, perhaps, to our self-esteem. It is that we may be willing today to give freedom to India, but that this is only the result of a belated recognition of past error, of a sense of our own incapacity to govern or defend India, of a death-bed repentance in face of overwhelming danger.

The underlying purpose of the speeches included in this little volume was to answer these charges. In these speeches I have attempted to set out the true nature of the freedom which we are fighting to defend in this world struggle, and more particularly of that British system of democratic freedom which we have, through the centuries, built up in this island, and since spread round the world, as well as to illustrate the particular features of the problem of completing the structure of freedom in India.

In the case of India, so far from depriving her of a pre-existing freedom and denying to her the opportunity of regaining it, we rescued her from the anarchy which is the last negation of freedom. We established, within the vast quadrilateral encompassed by her mountain ranges and twin seas, peace and order and the reign of law—the indispensable foundations of freedom. More than that, we inspired a passionate demand for a self-governing freedom which India had never known. How to meet that demand—as we must meet it and should gladly meet it—without sacrificing the foundations, how to transform an administrative unity into a self-sustaining, self-determining national life without a reversion to anarchy, that is a problem which cannot be solved by phrases or by irresponsible abdication, but only by constructive, tolerant statesmanship and patient good will.

To that task we have made our own contribution over the last generation or more. We have reached the stage when the main contribution must be made by Indians for themselves. We have laid the foundations; it is for them to plan and build the house in which they wish to live. That is the conclusion which for the last two years I have endeavoured to preach. That is the conclusion which Sir Stafford Cripps's mission, whatever its immediate results, has, I trust, finally brought home to the minds of India's political leaders.

In all this evolution of policy we have been true to our inherited instincts: our instinct for order, our reverence for law, our faith in freedom, our sense of realities. We have every right to be proud of what we have done in India. We have every right to be even more proud of what we are attempting to do in India. We have every right to hope that we shall, with Indian help, win through, not only the immediate issue of the war, but the more abiding issue of India's freedom and India's friendship.

In any case our share of that task is one which we should approach, not in any spirit of apology for the past, or of defeatism for the future, but in the proud and confident belief that the principles and instincts which have achieved the separate miracles of the creation of the present Indian Empire and of the evolution of the British Commonwealth of free nations will achieve the yet greater miracle of a partnership of freedom transcending and transforming both. We should approach it sustained, as Burke once bade us be sustained in approaching the problem of America, by the ancient motto of the Church: 'Sursum Corda'—with uplifted hearts.

L. S. AMERY

May 1942

CONTENTS

I

MAGNA CHARTA

BROADCAST JUNE 15TH, 1940

TODAY, June 15th, is the anniversary of the signing of Magna Charta. On this day 725 years ago our fathers established the foundations of English freedom. The detailed story of the events which led up to the great drama enacted at Runnymede is no doubt familiar to you all. You can picture for yourselves, far better than I can describe it for you, the scene on both banks of the river Thames and on the little island between: on the one side the crafty Angevin tyrant, furious but impotent, among his trembling foreign counsellors: on the other the embattled host of barons, great and small, the bishops and clerics, the mayor and citizens of London —that English nation, in fact, which unobserved had come into being in the century and a half since the Norman Conquest, and which was now for the first time to assert its power and its sagacity.

It was the power of the English people which exacted the great Charter. But it was its sagacity that refrained from a gratuitous assertion of power, which would have weakened the sovereign authority of the realm, and accepted King John's surrender in the form of a royal grant to his obedient subjects. It was that same sagacity which based the Charter, not on any claim of abstract right, but on the definite historical rights set out more than a century earlier in the Charter of Henry I and on the 'old Constitution of the realm'. It is, indeed, characteristic of the temper of our people that the great landmarks in our constitutional history, from Magna Charta to the Declaration of Rights, or the Statute of Westminster in our day, have taken the shape of a declaration of established and admitted principles rather than that of any assertion of something avowedly new. We have always been concerned, in Burke's words, 'to prove the pedigree of our liberties' and to prize them as 'an entailed inheritance derived to us from our forefathers'. At the same time we have been no less concerned to enlarge that inheritance, and these professed summaries of existing and acknowledged rights have, in each case, marked the starting point of new and fruitful developments.

This was true, above all, of Magna Charta. The whole system of our freedom, as it exists today, throughout the British Empire and in the United States, is founded on the 'Reign of Law', on the subjection of the Executive and of its Ministers and agents to the law of the land. The development of that system has taken centuries, but it is all there in essence in the famous article of Magna Charta which lays down 'that no free man shall be arrested, or detained in prison or outlawed or banished or brought to ruin, nor shall we set forth against him nor send against him, save by the judgement of his peers and in accordance with the law of the land'. Again what a potent germ was the article which provided that 'no scutage or aid shall be imposed save by the Common Council of the Realm'! For out of it grew Parliament, and through centuries to come it provided the all-powerful lever by which Parliament steadily increased its control over the whole machinery of government. It was to this principle of 'no taxation without representation' that the American colonies appealed in their struggle with the British Parliament. Their Constitution since then has developed on somewhat different lines from ours. But Magna Charta and the principles which were implicit in it are our common heritage and are still a living bond between us.

It was no theoretical freedom that the barons at Runnymede claimed for themselves and for a whole nation, but the truer freedom which comes from the enforcement of the law on all without regard to privilege or power, from the certainty of just and speedy decisions in the Courts, from protection against arbitrary taxation. Liberty is, indeed, a meaningless thing except as a right adjustment between all the forces and elements in the national life. That adjustment must vary continuously with changing circumstances, and continuously demands fresh methods to preserve it. A century ago we reformed the franchise in order to secure the liberty of trade and industry for the mercantile and industrial middle class against the domination of a landed oligarchy. We have extended it again and again since then in order to secure the liberty of the wage earner against the oppression of an unregulated capitalism. We have given woman a new position in the State in order to enlist her help against the tyranny of neglect in all those social questions that most closely touch her life and that of the home. But franchise itself is not freedom, nor is mere majority rule, regardless of circumstances, true democracy. A universal suffrage based on mere geographical constituencies may easily lead us to the most odious of class or party tyrannies. There can be no true freedom where each element, each function, in the social and economic life of the nation is not represented in some proportion to its intrinsic importance to the community.

The same need for continuous adjustment has governed the development of British freedom overseas. The principle of responsible self-government in essentially local matters which was laid down in Lord Durham's memorable report has developed in the case of the Dominions to a full-grown national stature and a complete equality of status with the Mother Country. They are today in the fullest sense of the word independent nations. But they are more, as we are more, than ordinary isolated nations. How many nations are there whose nominal independence is not in fact seriously limited by the economic pressure of more powerful neighbours? How many have we not seen succumb in these last few years and weeks to sheer brutal aggression? Against these dangers the nations of the British Commonwealth can look to a partnership, free yet assured, to sustain their mutual welfare in peace and defend their liberties in war. By their free action they are showing today the price they set upon that partnership.

In their case full equality, full partnership, has already been achieved. In the case of India we have made manifest our sincere desire that she should, as a willing partner, attain to the same status in the British Commonwealth as is enjoyed by the Dominions or, for that matter, by ourselves. If there are obstacles, apart from the immediate urgencies of war, to the speedy fulfilment of that desire, they arise more from the inherent complexities in India's own internal religious, social, and historic structure, than from any reluctance on our part to hasten the transition from one control to the other. It is our genuine wish to help to bridge over existing differences and to enable Indians as soon as possible to play the vital part which they are entitled to play in devising the permanent framework of India's future Constitution. Where our own responsibility is no less vitally engaged is to see to it that in the inevitable period of transition from one control to the other the security and orderly government of a united India—the indispensable foundation of her freedom—should not be imperilled. That, too, is an end which we believe can best be secured not by dictation but by mutual agreement. The task before the leaders of India, as before ourselves, is one of the noblest, if also one of the most difficult, which statesmanship has ever essayed. It will need all the spirit of Magna Charta, its practical sense as well as its generosity, to make that task possible of achievement.

In all that I have said I have assumed that freedom is worth while. I have assumed that our highest aim is a national life which is something greater than any element in it, greater even than the State, and which can find room within itself for many independent manifestations of local and corporate activity, for the free expression and organization of opinion on all questions, as well as for the freedom of every individual to live his own life 'by no man's leave underneath the Law'. I have assumed that we are dedicated to the ideal of a free commonwealth in which national patriotism and the wider patriotism of the whole can find their fullest expression without any subordination of one to the other; in which free co-operation for defence, for trade, for the development of all that exalts and enriches human life can take the place of coercion, and in which no attempt is made to force the infinite diversity of its peoples into a common mould.

Is that assumption justified? Can a nation or a commonwealth based on these principles endure? Is freedom itself an ideal still worth pursuing? These are the questions which are at issue in the eyes of the world today. By the suppression of all freedom of political organization and thought, by the cultivation of a ruthless fanaticism of brute force, and of an unscrupulous thirst for domination, Hitler and his associates and confederates have built up an engine of mechanized military power more terrible than anything yet dreamt of, and have launched it upon a world ill-prepared for so wanton and merciless an onslaught. If that onslaught succeeds then it is the end of Magna Charta and all that it has stood for, not only here in Europe but across the Atlantic and to the farthest ends of Asia and of Africa, for the defeat of the Allies would mean not only the loss of their own freedom. It would mean the extinction of freedom, even as an ideal, among mankind. Everywhere men would turn to worship the new gods of arbitrary power, of racial arrogance and of mechanized thought. Everywhere freedom would be overthrown, and trampled underfoot by the 'Fifth Column' from within. On the anniversary of Magna Charta, looking back on the growth of ordered freedom over the centuries between, we know that such an outcome is unthinkable. At all hazards, at all costs, we must win. For us there can be no compromise, no truce, only victory—the victory which our fathers won seven hundred years ago.

II

WHAT WE ARE FIGHTING FOR

BLACKPOOL, AUGUST 11TH, 1940

IN the year behind us we have seen one nation after another—Poland, Denmark, Norway, Holland, Belgium—overrun and trampled under foot by the overwhelming might of the Nazi engine of war. Last of all we have seen the heroic French Army broken by sheer weight of machine power, as well as by its own faulty conception of modern war. Saddest of all, we have seen a great freedom-loving nation, in a moment of despair, reft of all courageous leadership, forgetting the vast resources still at its disposal, forgetting its pledges to its ally, and only concerned to find favour in the eyes of the conqueror—a vain hope indeed. Now we are left to face the coming storm alone. We are not afraid. Here in 'this fortress built by Nature for herself' we stand prepared and ready for whatever form the attack may take, for whatever new devilry our enemy may have prepared for our destruction. The trial of our nerve, of our endurance, will be stern. One thing I do know. If Hitler thinks our spirit can be broken by mere mass attack from the air upon our industries and our shipping he will find himself grievously mistaken. He has got to achieve far more than that to win this war. He has got to come over and take us; take us and break us as he has taken and broken the others. Let him try. If he does he will fail disastrously and his failure will bring the end of the war nearer than anything else could possibly do. But if the stakes are too high for him and he gives up the attempt, that, too, will be failure, and all the world will know that the tide has turned and that, sooner or later, his fate is sealed.

He may hope as a second-best plan, if he cannot destroy the British Empire here at the heart, to lop off some of its limbs. He may send his bombers and airborne troops to stiffen his half-hearted Italian allies in their attack upon Egypt and upon our whole position in the Middle East and in Africa. If he does, his men will meet not only a warm climate but a warm reception. In any case nothing that he can do in that quarter can protect the heart of Germany from our growing strength in the air. Thanks to the superior skill and daring of our airmen —thanks also to the superiority of the men who designed and made their machines—we have already, with greatly inferior numbers, inflicted far more damage upon our enemy than we have suffered. More and more, week by week, as our resources in the air multiply, we shall seek the enemy out in his own home and destroy, one by one, the factories upon which his war power is based, the means of transport by which his armies and the life of his people are sustained. He has brutally seized half a continent, merely to serve as a vantage ground from which to attack us. Every point he has seized will soon prove a hostage to fortune, a target for our attack from the air, a frittering away of his forces upon the task of holding down peoples who only wait to rise against him when the hour of their deliverance approaches.

Meanwhile no continental conquests of his can shake off the stranglehold of our blockade. He may extend his empire for the time being. But more and more her conquered and oppressed peoples will look to us to deliver them alike from political enslavement and from dire material need. Then, masters of the sea and of the air, with our armies equipped and trained for the task, no longer of defence, but of deliverance, we shall—by what approach, with what allies, no one can yet say—seek out the dragon in his lair and put an end to this evil horror which today obsesses the world.

An evil horror, for it is, indeed, that and nothing else, that we are fighting against. Behind this terrible German engine of destruction, behind these armoured divisions, and millions of infantry, these serried air squadrons and lurking submarines, whose efficiency we cannot but admire, there lies a purpose as cruel and brutal as it is senseless, the mere lust for power as a means for yet further aggression. The Nazi creed which inspires that purpose is one which exalts cruelty and brutality, which despises mercy, tolerance, fair dealing and justice. It denies all moral obligations as between nations. It denies all rights to the individual as against the handful of gangsters who claim to represent the omnipotent State. It has often been said that the victory of Nazidom would mean the destruction of all the spiritual and moral heritage of our Western Christian civilization. So far as Europe is concerned that is true. We are heirs of a civilization to which ancient Greece gave the love of intellectual and political freedom, to which Rome gave the sense of law and order, to which Christianity contributed that reverence for the underlying equality of every individual human being before God, to which medieval chivalry added the regard for honour between equals, courtesy to women and pity for the weak. The Nazi creed denies and despises all these things. But ours is not the only civilization or the only religion. It is my privilege to serve in the British Government the interests of the Empire of India. The 350 million people of India can claim a civilization more ancient even than ours. They belong to religions which differ from ours in many aspects, but are at one with ours in their recognition of the spiritual value of the individual soul, in their reverence for a moral law which knows no boundaries of race and applies alike to rulers and ruled. There is no common meeting ground between Nazism, on the one side, and, on the other, Islam, with its profoundly democratic sense of equality, with its emphasis on mercy and pity for the poor and the weak, or Hinduism with its concentration on the spiritual side of life and its rejection of violence. It is not only our civilization and our religion here in Europe, but all civilization and all true religion that are threatened by the barbaric forces of spiritual even more than material destruction which are embodied in Nazi Germany today.

That is what we are fighting against. What are we fighting to maintain ? We speak of this war, and rightly, as a fight for freedom. But what do we mean by freedom ? We mean the freedom of nations, their right to live in their own way, to develop their own culture, their own political traditions. We think of the freedom of minorities, their right to follow, undisturbed and unpersecuted, their own religion, their own language, their own individuality. We think of the freedom of the individual citizen, man or woman, to attain to the fullest growth of mind and heart, not at the expense of others, but in co-operation with them. Above all, perhaps, we think of the freedom of the individual to contribute, by speech or pen or vote, his share of service to the common good.

In no country in the world has that freedom found so full and varied an expression as here. Through the centuries, from Magna Charta onwards, we have built it up by free discussion, sometimes even in bitter conflict. It has become a tradition, deep ingrained in our very natures, a precious inheritance without which life itself would not be worth living for Englishmen. We are fighting, and will fight to the death, to maintain it. But we are fighting for something more, for the right and opportunity to continue enlarging and enriching our freedom. No one can say that even here freedom has yet reached its fullest flowering. Political freedom and equality we have achieved, though it will still need eternal vigilance to preserve it. But we have still much to do if we are to win for our people as a whole that greater freedom and equality in their economic lives, that sense of security that we wish to see them attain. The ideal of a Merrie England in which every boy and girl will grow up in happy and healthy home surroundings, in which they will enjoy every opportunity for the equal development of their minds and bodies so as to become true men and women, living their own lives to the full and contributing to the full, as citizens, to the welfare and happiness of others—that is a future for which all the sacrifices of the present are well worth while. To attain that ideal we shall all have to contribute our share of effort and sacrifice. But it will be a small and easy thing compared with what we are called upon to do and suffer in this struggle, if only we preserve after the war that spirit of brotherhood which holds us together today. Material resources will be there in abundance, increased, in spite of the waste of war, by the new vigour and new methods war will have taught us, so long as we do not relapse, as we did before, into selfishness and complacency.

This English freedom of ours we have never thought of as a monopoly to be secured for ourselves at the expense of others. We have sought to spread it, wherever our adventurous people have wandered afield, wherever British influence has extended. It has been the life blood of our Empire, securing unfailing allegiance across the wide world spaces, converting conquest into free and equal partnership. Amid all the world changes of the last century, the crash of falling empires and the noisy emergence of new nations, nothing has been more remarkable than the almost unobserved growth of the British emigrant colonies overseas into great nations, not by secession or disruption, but by a willing enlargement of freedom which has strengthened our Commonwealth as it has imperceptibly transformed it.

That has been a wonderful experiment, and we see the fruits of its success in the Dominion Armies which have come here and to every threatened point in the Empire to defend our common freedom and our common cause. We are engaged upon the even more daring experiment of applying the same principles to India, with her many races and creeds, with her immensely complex political structure, with her difficult and dangerous problems of defence. I have no doubt we shall succeed, because, in the long run, good will, sincerity and statesmanship on both sides must prevail over shortsighted fears and suspicions. We have repeatedly declared our resolve that India shall attain to the same freedom, to the same full and equal partnership in the Commonwealth, as the other Dominions or, for that matter, as this country itself. There is no greater freedom, no higher status, than that in the world today. We have, in these last few days, given further earnest of our intentions by making it clear that, subject to due provision for those special obligations and responsibilities which our long connexion with India has imposed upon us, we wish to see India, like the other Dominions, framing her own Constitution in her own way, and in harmony with her own political, social, and economic conceptions. And if that can only be finalized after the war is over there is nothing to prevent much indispensable preliminary work of study and discussion and negotiation being taken in hand by friendly agreement even during the war. Nor could anything help that atmosphere of friendly agreement more than the acceptance by Indian leaders of all political parties of their share in the work of government, making it in fact, in India as we have made it here, a truly national government enjoying the good will and confidence of all the main elements in India's national life. India is united today in her detestation of Nazi tyranny and Nazi aggression. She knows the menace which a Nazi victory would mean, not only to the fabric of the British Empire as a whole, but to India's own existence, to her political aspirations, to her moral and spiritual ideals. I can only hope and trust that, realizing this, her political leaders will accept, without prejudice and in the spirit that it has been offered to them, the opportunity of serving the immediate interest of India in the world struggle, and thus pave the way, most smoothly and speedily, towards the realization of the goal to which we and they equally aspire.

Nor is our desire for the spread of freedom confined to our own Commonwealth. We believe that within that Commonwealth freedom means strength, security, and prosperity. But we believe that freedom in the world anywhere means friendship for us and makes for peace. We wish to see the peoples of Europe united together after this war in free co-operation for their mutual security and welfare. We do not fear that result. A Europe united under the domination of an aggressor must always be a threat to ourselves and to the rest of humanity. A Europe united in freedom can only make for that general peace which we have always recognized as one of the first of British interests. Its prosperity, its social well-being, can only contribute to ours. It is because that is our faith and the mainspring of our actions that all who love freedom in Europe will continue to look to us to break asunder the bars of the prison in which they are now confined and to bring them the succour and relief of which they stand so sorely in need.

They may not have long to wait. The effort that Hitler has imposed upon the German people to prepare for his overwhelming blow, his blitzkrieg, against his neighbours has been out of all proportion to their permanent resources and staying power. Freedom may be careless and slow to realize danger. But it has a staying and a creative power, and an enduring flame of passion, that are bound to outlive and gain the mastery over mechanized preparations, however elaborate, and over mechanized minds, however diligent and docile. Knowing that, we can face with unshakably serene confidence whatever terrors the next few weeks may bring us here at home, whatever efforts and sacrifices may yet be required to regain lost ground in Europe or overseas. Sooner or later, at some unexpected moment, in some yet unexpected way, the empire built of hatred and contempt of all moral law, will agonize and dissolve and we shall wake from the nightmare of war to find that we have once again saved ourselves by our exertions, and the world by our example. Meanwhile, in the assured faith of our victory, and of the new birth of freedom we shall win for ourselves and for others, let us rise to the height of this, the greatest occasion in our history, and show ourselves worthy, not only of our great past, but of our greater future.

III

OUR INDIAN RECORD

ENGLISH SPEAKING UNION, NOVEMBER 21ST, 1940

Of all achievements of the British genius the creation of the British Empire of India is the most spectacular. It may yet—if we can see our task through to its fulfilment—prove the most significant for the future of the world. No romance can compare with the story of the handful of Englishmen—never more than a handful—who, beginning as mere traders and merchant settlers, have in barely two centuries built up the majestic structure of an Imperial system under which peace, order and good government are secured for three hundred and fifty millions of human beings of many races and creeds inhabiting what is in essence a continent of its own. For India is truly a continent, a definite region of the world, in at least the same sense as Europe. She is not less in extent or population than the real Europe, which begins west of Russia. She is more sharply separated from the rest of the great Eur-Asiatic land mass. She is inhabited by a no less distinctive breed of men.

In one sense, indeed, India is much more 'continental' than Europe, which is mainly 'peninsular', lending itself to natural sub-division and to the growth of self-contained nationalities. India, within the rough quadrilateral of her mountains and seas, has no natural internal frontiers. That is the fundamental historic and political feature of the Indian problem. Her successive conquerors have inevitably tended and striven to extend their racial, religious, or political influence over the whole, and those influences are today inextricably intertwined from the Himalayas to Cape Comorin. Only in political unity can India find peace and stability. That was why India accepted the alien rule of the Moguls. That was why, after the almost unbelievable horrors of the century of anarchy which followed the breakdown of that rule, she welcomed the efficient, just, detached yet sympathetic administration that Englishmen were prepared to give her as circumstances progressively forced the responsibilities of Indian government upon them.

We gave to India the unity of government which was her first need. We gave it her in the only form in which she could then conceive of government, namely, government from above. The bureaucratic system which we established in India was not, as a type of government, alien to the ideas of the India which accepted it. Nor was the notion of a ruling race from outside essentially repugnant to peoples whose history, from earliest times to that of the Moguls, had accustomed them to racial ascendancy, and among whom caste—sprung originally from the same source—was an infinitely stronger influence than nationality. Yet, even from the start, we gave more than any of our predecessors. Our rule, if autocratic, was never arbitrary. Wherever it extended, British rule brought with it the reign of law, and India received almost simultaneously those first two stages in the development of ordered freedom which for us were marked by the Norman Conquest and by the granting of Magna Charta. And if we did not, and could not, give India British political institutions at the outset, we made them inevitable in the long run by our gift of the English language, the strongest unifying force in India, not merely as a common medium but as the common foundation of all political thinking among Indians of every race and every creed.

Macaulay, indeed, who initiated the system of English education in India looked to it as leading some day to the demand for English institutions, and claimed that when that day came it would be 'the proudest day in English history'. In principle, at least, we have from the very first encouraged India to look to self-government as her proper and rightful destiny within the British family. In practice, for the half-century which followed the establishment of the direct rule of the Crown after the Mutiny, we were too intent on the immediate efficiency of administration to face the political problems of the future, and to prepare for them by a progressive opening of the field for Indian executive and legislative responsibility. On the contrary, the whole tendency was to eliminate such elements of indigenous self-government as still survived by a direct rule whose greatest merit, the personal authority of the individual English district officer, became, in its turn, more and more submerged by the routine of an over-centralized bureaucracy. It was only after the turn of the century that Lord Minto, a Conservative statesman with Dominion experience, became convinced and was able to convince a Liberal Government that Indian political aspirations were a real and permanent force and one to which some effective constitutional expression must be given. India and the Empire owe much to Lord Minto's insight and generous sympathy. He was the first to appoint an Indian to the Viceroy's Council, and to make a beginning of the opening to Indians of a career in the officer ranks of the Indian Army. The Morley-Minto reforms of 1909 enlarged the existing Legislative Councils, and, in the provinces at least, established non-official and largely elected majorities.

The Morley-Minto reforms were the first response to the growing nationalist movement in India itself. The origins of that movement go back to the creation of the Indian National Congress in 1885. Beginning on purely constitutional and moderate lines the Congress movement had by the early years of the present century taken on a much more aggressive and even extremist aspect. At the same time its claim to represent all India became less and less acceptable to the bulk of Moslem opinion. Even the distant approach of self-government began to awaken in the Moslem community, more than a quarter of the whole population of India, the consciousness of the profound differences separating it from the Hindu majority and the instinctive determination not to exchange British rule for Hindu majority rule. In 1906 the All-Indian Moslem League was formed and was soon after in a position to secure from a profoundly reluctant Secretary of State the right to separate communal representation under the new reforms. But no one at the time realized how far-reaching were the implications of this admission of the permanent division between the two communities or how inconsistent it was with the conscious or instinctive tendency towards following the course of constitutional development in the relatively homogeneous Dominions.

Meanwhile the reforms undoubtedly went a good way towards meeting moderate Indian opinion. At the same time they created on the British side, in India and here, a readiness to favour further progress. This disposition was greatly strengthened by a sincere appreciation of the invaluable contribution Indian loyalty and Indian valour rendered in the course of the last war. More than a year before the end of that war the British War Cabinet, headed by Mr Lloyd George and including not only Lord Balfour and Lord Milner, but also one who has always been regarded as the last embodiment of the old regime in India, Lord Curzon, defined its Indian policy in Mr Montagu's famous pronouncement as:

> 'The increasing association of Indians in every branch of the administration and the gradual development of self-governing institutions with a view to the progressive realization of responsible government in India as an integral part of the British Empire'.

The first step in the new policy was the Government of India Act of 1919 under which the administration of the Provincial Governments in respect of all except the 'reserved' subjects of finance and law and order was transferred to Indian Ministers chosen from and responsible to the majority of the greatly enlarged Provincial Legislative Councils. The Act at the same time converted the Governor-General's nominated Legislative Council at the Centre into a bicameral legislature in which over half of the Upper House and over two-thirds of the Lower House were elected.

The new regime started badly. India, like all the rest of the world, went through a period of unrest in the reaction after the war. In India, that unrest took a shape peculiarly its own and characteristically Indian, largely through the personality of Mr Gandhi, a remarkable blend of saint, idealist, and astute party leader. His policy of non-violent passive resistance to Government rapidly degenerated into mob violence with its regrettable but inevitable sequel of repression. For all that, both at the Centre and in the Provinces, as well as in the gradual Indianization of the civil and military services, the new policy established itself. In 1927 the appointment of the Simon Commission was a recognition of the fact that the time for a further constitutional advance was at hand.

The Report of the Commission was noteworthy for two main conclusions. The first was that the Provinces were ripe for full responsible self-government, including the administration of law and order. The other was that British India, as such, was utterly unsuited to provide the foundation of any permanent system of self-government. So long as bureaucracy was in control, and could in a measure look after the interests of the Indian States as well as of British India, it mattered little that the two Indias—geographically and economically inextricably interlocked, and forming together the only natural unity that India possesses, the unity of the whole sub-continent—were under two separate systems of government. To create a self-governing Dominion of British India—the natural sequel of the Montague-Chelmsford Central Government—would be to bring about a wholly indefensible partition of an essential unity, and to put the States into an impossible position. An All-India Federation was, therefore, in the Commission's opinion, the only ultimate solution of the problem, and it was to this that all their marshalling of facts and of arguments irresistibly pointed.

I need not detain you with the proceedings of those sessions of the Round Table Conference and of the Joint Select Committee of Parliament which followed up the recommendations implicit in the Simon Report and culminated in the India Act of 1935. In those prolonged discussions Indian statesmen took an active part—though Congress, apart from one brief and unfruitful attendance by Mr Gandhi, decided to abstain—and the credit for the final shaping of the measure should rightly go to them as well as to British statesmen and to Parliament. The Act was a remarkable feat of constructive statesmanship. It established in the eleven provinces of British India a complete system of democratic self-government on British Parliamentary lines for a wide range of subjects. At the same time it set up the framework for a federal system joining together these Provinces with such of the Indian States as chose to come within its purview.

At the Centre, as well as in the Provinces, the Act provided, subject to certain detailed safeguards, for Parliamentary Responsible Government in respect of all subjects save Defence and Foreign Policy which are reserved for the Viceroy's direct control through counsellors responsible to him alone. For the rest Indian Ministers were to be responsible to a Legislature carefully balanced so as to adjust the competing claims of Provinces and States and making special provision for communal representation both for Moslems and for the Scheduled Castes or so-called 'Untouchables'.

Congress denounced the Act as wholly inadequate and unacceptable, but in the end accepted the responsibility of taking office in the seven out of eleven Provinces in which it had secured an electoral majority. In the other Provinces Moslem-Hindu coalitions were set up and are still in successful operation today. The Congress Ministers themselves govern not unsuccessfully, though not without some difficulty in attempting to reconcile extravagant election pledges with the practical necessities of administration. But their exclusion from office of representatives of the minority elements, on the conventional democratic theory that they merely represented the 'beaten party', and the whole spirit of the Congress system created increasing mistrust among those elements, as well as among the Indian Princes; an alarm which was naturally intensified when at the outbreak of the present war, the Congress Executive ordered reluctant Ministers in the Congress Provinces to resign. Even in more or less homogeneous countries, it is doubtful whether parliamentary democracy can flourish once the real centre of power is transferred from Parliament and Ministry to an outside caucus. In the circumstances of India that danger is accentuated, not only by the presence of wholly inassimilable elements outside the Party machine, but also by the fact that those who control Congress sincerely regard themselves as the only possible instrument of India's political emancipation and conceive their mission with a religious fervour which dismisses all opposition as reactionary or factious and rejects all compromise.

Whether the Federal provisions of the Act might have worked if brought into operation promptly is, perhaps, an open question. What is certain is that the delays involved, and the experience of Congress government in the Provinces, have raised new and formidable issues which make the enforcement of the Act at the Centre impossible without considerable modification or even fundamental reconstruction. Congress has rejected these provisions of the Act both because they still retain British control of defence and foreign policy and because the voting power assigned to the States violates their theories of strict arithmetical democracy. They have demanded a new Constitution to be framed by an Indian Constituent Assembly based on universal suffrage all over India, including the Indian States.

The Moslem objection to the recent Act, namely, that it would always put power into the hands of a Hindu (if not necessarily a Congress majority) is, of course, infinitely stronger against any kind of Constitution that could emerge from a Congress-controlled Constituent Assembly. Their answer to the Congress demand is that they would sooner go outside of India altogether and set up an independent Pakistan composed of the north-western and north-eastern Provinces in which Moslems constitute a majority. The Princes, whose earlier disposition to join the scheme of federation embodied in the Act had already been profoundly affected by the Congress attitude of the last few years, could naturally not be expected to agree to the Congress proposals or to join in with any India constituted on Congress lines.

The constitutional deadlock today is not between a

constituent Indian national movement asking for freedom and a British Government reluctant to surrender its authority, but between the main elements in India's own national life. The problem is not how to hasten on the devolution of that authority to willing Indian hands, but how to find a constitutional solution which will preserve, in some practical degree at least, the unity of India and avert a process of internal disintegration to which it might be impossible to set a limit, and which would certainly put an end to all hopes of real democracy and real social progress.

The answer to the problem is, in the first instance at any rate, for Indians themselves to provide. The British Government can help, no doubt, and must help. But the primary responsibility for solving India's internal relationships should rest upon those Indians who are capable of thinking in terms of 'India First' and not of any one community, state or party organization. The capacity to solve a problem of this character by constructive device and fair compromise has, after all, in the United States 150 years ago, and in the British Dominions more recently, afforded the true test of fitness for a full national life. It is with these considerations in view that the Viceroy on August 8th issued the declaration of policy which he again briefly recapitulated yesterday.[1] In that declaration His Majesty's Government affirmed its sympathy with the idea that the framing of India's future Constitution should rest with Indians themselves and originate from Indian conceptions of the social, economic and political structure of Indian life. That acceptance of one part at least of the Congress demand was subject to two conditions. One was the due fulfilment of the obligations which Great Britain's long connexion with India has imposed on her and for which His Majesty's Government cannot divest themselves of responsibility. Of that condition I shall say a word in a moment. The other was that the new Constitution must arise from agreement between the main elements in India's national life and that His Majesty's Govern-

[1] See Appendix I.

ment could not contemplate the transfer of their present responsibilities for the peace and welfare of India to any system of government whose authority is directly denied by large and powerful elements in India's national life. Subject to these vital conditions we have expressed our willingness that such a new Constitution shall be decided by a representative body based on agreement and come into operation with the least possible delay after the war. Meanwhile we are prepared to welcome and promote in any way possible every sincere and practical step that may be taken by representative Indians to reach agreement upon the form of the post-war representative body and upon the principles and outlines of the future Constitution itself.

As an interim measure the declaration expressed the desire of His Majesty's Government that the political leaders of India should be given the opportunity of more direct, responsible association with the conduct of India's government during the war, by the expansion of the Viceroy's Executive and the formation of an All-India War Advisory Council. Our hope was, not only that Indian leaders should as the heads of great national departments gain experience in the responsibilities of government, but also that in the process of working together new bonds of union and understanding might emerge between them and thus pave the way to the solution of those internal differences which are the real obstacles to India's constitutional progress.

This latter hope has not, I regret to say, been fulfilled at any rate for the time being. Congress has rejected the Government's offer, root and branch, not only as regards the interim proposals but as regards the constitutional method of advance for the future, and has decided to embark on a campaign of protest in the shape of speeches defying the law by directly urging the people of India to refuse to enlist, or produce munitions or subscribe to war funds. That campaign is a matter for the administration and the law courts to deal with and I need not discuss it here. Outside Congress I think I can fairly say that India as a whole welcomed the major constitutional solution. All the so-called minority elements at any rate have seen in it an assurance that they are entitled to have their voice in the future shaping of India's national life and are not to be handed over behind their backs to Congress by a British Government wearied by the difficulties and complexities of the Indian problem. It is true that as regards the interim solution they, too, have made difficulties over details which have decided the Viceroy for the time being to suspend the expansion of his executive and the formation of the proposed War Advisory Council. That is a matter of genuine regret. It means that at a most critical and creative moment in India's national life, Indian leaders have not been ready to sink their differences, or to face responsibility towards their followers with sufficient courage, to avail themselves of a real opportunity for the exercise of responsible power and influence, for the practical advance of India towards full Dominion status.

That, however, is but an incident, and in any case the door remains open for reconsideration. What I am concerned to make clear to you is that the main problem before India now is to discover a solution for her own internal structure which will meet the essential requirements of all parties and yet preserve in its main essentials at any rate an India united in its relation to the outside world. The problem of the further concession of India's claim to self-government is now a secondary one, because it has in fact been conceded in principle, and the limitations imposed upon it are imposed, not by British reluctance to surrender control, but by the ineluctable circumstances of India's external and internal relations. In the case of the Dominions the process of disentanglement between British and local authority was an easy and rapid one. Their geographical isolation and the automatic protection afforded by a then all powerful British Navy made their problems of defence matters of minor consequence which they could easily maintain unaided, and relieved them from all serious pre-occupation with foreign policy. India's position in these respects has been entirely different. Both for internal peace and for external security we have had to build up in India a powerful military system based mainly upon an Indian Army, hitherto mainly officered and directed by British officers, together with a considerable force of British troops. Even these could not hope to defend India against aggression from Russia or Japan without reinforcement from the rest of the Empire.

If India were declared independent to-morrow she could only gradually and over a period of years dispense with this outside support to her defensive structure and it is obviously inconceivable that this country should put its forces at India's disposal without some say as to the use made of them or the foreign policy which might involve that use. Only the growth of India's power to provide unaided for her own defence can free her from at any rate some measure of interlocking between British and Indian foreign and military policy. Similar considerations apply to such other aspects of the situation as the position and rights of the Indian States to which there is no parallel in the case of the Dominions. There is, however, nothing in these inherent limitations, temporary or more enduring, which need imply any impairment of status, or any derogation from those 'principles of equality and similarity appropriate to status' which, as Lord Balfour explained in his remarkable exposition of the nature of the British Commonwealth in the Constitutional Report of the Imperial Conference of 1926, 'do not universally extend to function'. In any case the real difficulty is not one of lack of good will towards India's attainment of that full and equal partnership in the British Commonwealth which is not only the 'proclaimed and accepted goal of the Imperial Crown and of the British Parliament' but the highest status and greatest measure of security and independence to which any nation can hope to attain.

To return to the main issue which is the problem of finding an Indian Constitution which can reconcile Indian differences and preserve an India united at any rate in essentials, we naturally ask what is it that is wrong with the Constitution so carefully devised during all the discussions which preceded the Act of 1935? Is it the extent of the powers retained at the Centre? Is it the methods of representation? Or is it Parliamentary Government itself, in the sense of an executive depending directly and from day to day upon the support of a parliamentary majority—and in the absence of a strong parliamentary tradition to the contrary, upon a party executive behind that majority? The present deadlock is in the main the result of instinctive development, along the lines which our peculiar history and local conditions have made successful in this country and in the Dominions, in the wholly different and far more complex conditions of India. Only the most frank and far-reaching reconsideration of the methods we and they have been accustomed to take for granted may help Indians to solve their problem, and in doing so they can well afford to study other constitutional precedents than our own.

It may be that the fears of the Moslems might be largely met by a further increase in the powers of the Provinces, possibly rearranged and regrouped, subject only to the minimum of central control necessary to secure some measure of unity in foreign, defensive, and economic policy. A change in that direction would no doubt also largely meet the hesitations of the Princes. It would still, of course, involve some central executive and some central legislature empowered to vote and levy the necessary expenses. It may be that other forms of representation, e.g., functional representation, such as has already been tentatively established in some Indian States might greatly help to get over the communal difficulty. Lastly it may be that our whole conception of a Parliamentary Executive is, for the Central Government of India, at any rate, less suited than an Executive more on American lines, i.e., independent of the Legislature for the term of its office, whether directly elected or nominated by the Provinces and States, and with definite proportions allocated to the different main elements.

It is, I believe, for Indians themselves to face these questions and seek for a constructive solution. It may well be that the lead in such a study will come, not so much from the older party leaders who have naturally spun themselves into the cocoon of their own past controversies with the government and with each other, but from the younger men who are inspired with a patriotism which puts India first, not only before subservience to Britain, but also before subservience to party or community. My appeal would be to them, to the great Indian universities, as well as to responsible and thoughtful men in the practical and business world of India to get together for the study of the infinitely difficult and yet infinitely hopeful problem which India presents. After all to build an enduring constitutional framework in which 350 and more million people can live in freedom and at the same time in unity and peace with each other and in security against the outside world—that would be an achievement to which history so far affords no real parallel. If Indians can achieve that they can well afford to be proud of their achievement. If we have laid the foundation, material and spiritual, for that achievement we also can well afford to look back with honourable satisfaction upon the part we have played in India's life.

IV

INDIA FIRST

FOYLE LUNCHEON CLUB, DECEMBER 12TH, 1940

IT is of the essence of politics in our democratic age that it is largely governed by slogans, by simple words or phrases which sum up a principle, a method or a purpose which can be applied to almost every situation, and which gain strength by constant reiteration. Is there such a slogan or watchword which can effectively be applied to the affairs of India in this present difficult juncture, and applied not only by Indians of every community or section in their relations to each other or to the British Government, but also by Englishmen, whether here or in India, in their outlook upon the Indian problem, and afford equally helpful guidance to all of us ? I believe there is, and I am going to be bold enough to submit it for your consideration here, and not for your consideration only, but also, if my words and their sincere purpose carry that far, to Indians in their own country. That watchword is 'India First'. Let me say to begin with what I mean by the word 'India'. By India I mean India as a whole; India as nature and history have shaped her; India with her infinite diversity and underlying unity, India as she is today and as we wish her to be in the years to come.

Let us first look at nature's handiwork. A glance at the map is enough to show that India is truly a continent, a definite region of the world, in at least as true a sense as Europe, and far more sharply separated from the main block of the Old World. On the other hand, unlike Europe which is naturally broken up into self-contained units, India, within the quadrilateral of her mighty mountain ranges and spacious seas, has no natural internal frontiers, no natural barriers behind which clearly separated nationalities could grow up and live their several mainly self-regarding lives.

History, in its turn, has inevitably conformed to the ground-plan laid by nature. India, like our own island, has submitted to many influences from without. Wave after wave of invaders has swept down upon her through her north-western gateway, no doubt even before the days of the fair-skinned northern pastoralists who gave to most of India her Aryan speech and her most characteristic religious philosophy. For a thousand years Islam penetrated and permeated India not only as a conquering but as a proselytizing force. None of these influences found any natural barrier to arrest them. They remained strongest, no doubt, in the regions they first entered, but in varying degrees they spread in every direction to India's furthest confines. Hinduism and Islam, in very varying proportions, are conterminous over the whole sub-continent. What is more, in the process history has created in India, in spite of infinite variations in detail, variations everywhere shading insensibly into each other, her own distinctive human type, and in large measure her own distinctive way of life.

Last, but in some respects most potent of all these external influences has been that of this country, exercised upon India now for nearly three hundred years. Its effect upon India's racial composition and internal social structure has been negligible. But in the political domain the effect has far exceeded that of any of its predecessors. Every previous rule in India had inevitably attempted to extend its authority over India as a whole. British rule alone succeeded in giving India that political unity which is the indispensable condition of her free and peaceful development. It gave to India what the Norman Conquest gave England, a strong, ordered administration. It gave what England won for herself in Magna Charta, the Reign of Law, and a legal system to which Indian judges and lawyers have progressively contributed, to administer and to enrich. It gave, above all, in the English language, not only a common medium, but a common foundation of political thinking among Indians of every class or creed. In that sense at least the British influence in India has become an integral part of her national life and India and England are today, in political outlook and aspiration, if not in race, members of one political family.

What I want to emphasize is that these things, the political unity of India and the development in India of British conceptions of individual freedom and national self-government, are intimately connected. The internal unity and peace enforced by the strong hand of our early Norman kings and the external security afforded by our insular position were in no small measure responsible for the growth of freedom in this country, just as the absence of clearly defined frontiers, racial or geographical, has fostered autocracy and militarism in Central Europe. Once broken up into separate independent entities India would relapse, as it did in the decline of the Mogul Empire, into a welter of contending powers, in which free institutions would inevitably be suppressed, and in which no one element would have the resources with which to defend itself against external attack whether by land or by sea.

I have tried to explain what I mean by India. What then do I mean by 'India First'? I think I can best convey my meaning in alternative ways, putting myself in the place, first of one and then of another of those to whom I wish to commend this watchword. Let me begin by placing myself in the position of a British Indian, a member of the Hindu community, a believer in Indian freedom from outside control and in democracy —shall I say a follower of Congress or of the Mahasabha? What should 'India First' mean for one in that position? How in that case should I interpret it for myself? Would it not be in some such sense as follows: 'If I put India first, then must I not win over to my conception of India's future my Moslem neighbour who is as essentially and necessarily a part of India as I am? I may prefer a democratic system on the simple majority basis that prevails in England, and a closely knit centralized Constitution. But should those preferences stand in the way of some compromise which would enable him to feel that his community will as surely enjoy, in the future India, as real a freedom and as full a development of its individual communal and cultural entity as my own? I may dislike autocracy: but should I therefore exclude from Indian unity and Indian autonomy States which are an indispensable part of that unity and which in their way of life and traditions are the most characteristically Indian parts of India, rather than welcome them and trust to time and example to bring about the changes which I might desire?'

On the other hand, if I put myself in the shoes of an Indian Moslem how should I then interpret 'India First'? Would it not be in some such wise: 'Bound as I am to assert the right of my own community to be recognized as a permanent element in India's national life, and not as a mere numerical minority, am I entitled to push that claim to the point of imposing a veto on all political progress except at the cost of a complete break up of Indian unity which would be equally disastrous to us both?' What again would be the meaning of 'India First' to the ruler of an Indian State? Would it not be something to this effect: 'Much as I prize the privileged and secure position assured to me by my treaty with the Imperial Crown, sincerely as I believe that my long-established methods of government make for the welfare of my people, have I not a special obligation as a natural leader in India to make my contribution to Indian unity by the sacrifice of some of my sovereign powers and by such reforms in the internal Constitution of my own State as will bring it more nearly in harmony with the political life of India as a whole?' From every element in India the watchword 'India First' demands comprehension, tolerance, compromise; acceptance of the real India as its exists today, not the uncompromising insistence upon the immediate and complete realization of the theoretical India which any particular element or party has inscribed upon its banner.

So far I have spoken of the issue as affecting the relations between the different elements within India itself. What of the relation between India and Britain? What should 'India First' mean either to an Indian in relation to the British Commonwealth or to an Englishman in his relation to the affairs of India? Should it, for an Indian, mean partnership in that Commonwealth or severance from it? Let me answer that question by first putting another. What would 'Britain First' mean to me as an Englishman? My own immediate duty is to my own country, to do what I can to make Britain prosperous, secure, honoured among the nations, exercising her influence for freedom, peace, and progress in the world. At the same time I know that nothing can contribute more to every one of these objects than the continuance and development of that free co-operation with nations essentially kindred in outlook and ideas which is the foundation of our British Commonwealth. The maintenance of that Commonwealth means for us the enlargement, as severance would spell the diminution of our freedom. Is it otherwise with India? Is that security which 'India First' implies even possible for India except in assured reliance upon some wider partnership? And where could India find a partnership more effective in its support, less exacting in its demands, and, above all, more concordant in its character with India's innate spiritual outlook as well as with the political outlook which the centuries of British influence have implanted in her leaders?

Nor is there any conflict between the claims upon my conduct, or that of any other Englishman, in his relation to Indian affairs, of 'Britain First' and of 'India First'. Believing as I do that the highest interest of Britain lies in the strength and permanence of the British Commonwealth, I know that the strength of that Commonwealth, the permanence of that Commonwealth, can only be based on the fullest freedom, the fullest development, the fullest variety of individual life in each of its parts.

I think I can claim in all sincerity that it was from that point of view that the Viceroy made a memorable statement three months ago. That statement outlined the procedure by which Indians can arrive at the agreed framework of India's future Constitution. It offered, to Indian political leaders, as an immediate instalment, as wide an effective participation in the government of India as is practicable under the conditions of the present struggle for existence, and with the basis for an agreed Constitution still wholly unsettled. That offer has for the moment been rejected, not because it was in itself inadequate, but because the spirit of 'India First', the spirit of agreement, of compromise, of a recognition of realities, was not strong enough to overcome the insistence on unpractical demands on one side or undue suspicion on the other. I am not prepared to believe that this will be India's final reaction to the offer which is still before her. There must be many, of every party and every community in India, younger men with ideals and yet wide-eyed for reality, men of ability prepared to grapple with the sheer intellectual difficulties of the problem, practical men of affairs accustomed to give and take, who between them, by patient study and frank discussion, should be able to find a way out of a deadlock between contending Indian claims which cannot serve either India or that common cause in the present conflict which every Indian knows is as much his own as it is ours. It is to them above all that I would commend the watchword of 'India First' which I have made my theme to you here today.

THE INDIAN CONSTITUTIONAL PROBLEM

MANCHESTER LUNCHEON CLUB, NOVEMBER 19TH, 1941

Few problems have ever confronted human statesmanship more important, more complex or more difficult than that of India's future after this war. The task with which its solution confronts alike British and Indian statesmanship is tremendous. Those of us who have to play any part, however small, in dealing with it can only approach it with a certain awe at the thought of their responsibility and not without a deep sense of humility. In saying that I am not suggesting that we of this country should address ourselves to our share of the task in any spirit of apology for our own past record; far from it. We can well be proud of Britain's contribution to India. We have given her unity, peace within her borders, the all-pervading reign of impartial law. These are the indispensable foundations for the fulfilment of those ideals of political freedom which we have implanted in Indian minds. What the Norman Conquest gave us of effective central government, what Magna Charta won for us in the rights of the individual under the law, that we have given to India. That achievement itself was something of a miracle. We have now set ourselves to achieve, in co-operation with Indian statesmanship, the far greater miracle of building up in India, within the space of a few years, that superstructure of responsible freedom which we here took centuries after Magna Charta to complete—if, indeed, it can ever be said to be completed.

It is, indeed, essential if we are to have hope of success that we should have faith in ourselves, faith in our capacity and our courage, faith in the principles by which we have grown great, by which we live and for which we are fighting today. But faith and hope are not enough. We need also charity, good will, understanding, sympathy. We need good will towards Indian aspirations; I would say, indeed, that there is nothing more remarkable than the growth of that good will and understanding in Parliament and outside, in recent years. We need, no less, good will and understanding from Indians for our own endeavours. In spite of much criticism and suspicion we still, I believe, retain a real fund of underlying good will and confidence in India, as well as much personal good will between Indians and their British associates in administration or in business. Above all there is need for good will between Indians themselves. There, perhaps, lies the greatest difficulty and danger before India, and one which our particular form of democracy, with its rivalry for power between organized parties, has almost inevitably tended to accentuate. It is only by mutual good will, by the wider patriotism which puts India first, that it will be possible to find those compromises and adjustments without which no solution is possible.

But no less essential than good will is intellectual honesty, the facing of facts as they are. Good will need not mean loose thinking of easy sentimentality. The problem of India is not to be solved by catch phrases. 'We are fighting for democracy, why not therefore give India what she wants?' That sounds plausible and generous. But where is the body, in existence or yet to be constituted, which can in that sense speak for India or express an agreed demand? What form of democracy can be found under which the peoples of India are prepared to live together? The question brings us not a step nearer to the solution of our problem.

There could be no more typical instance of loose thinking than the clamour for what is called the application of the Atlantic Charter to India, and the protest against the Prime Minister's perfectly clear explanation that Article 3 of the Charter primarily referred to the restoration of national life in Europe and in any case did not qualify in any way our own declaration as to India's future with which it is in entire harmony. After all, what does that Article say? It says that among the principles on which the Prime Minister and Mr

Roosevelt base their hopes for a better future for the world is respect for the right of all peoples to choose the form of government under which they live. How far does that carry us with regard to India? It gives no indication as to whether India is to be regarded as one people or several; it does not say by what method the form of government is to be decided; it lays down no procedure, no time-table. On all these points it naturally does not attempt either to give guidance or impose any precise obligation. I can well imagine if, in answer to the demand for a statement of our Indian policy, we had answered merely in the terms of the Atlantic Charter, the derision and indignation which would have met so vague and unsatisfying a reply.

The answer we did give, in August of last year, was no less far reaching in its scope and far more definite in the procedure envisaged and in the pledge involved. It defined as our proclaimed and accepted goal that free and equal partnership in the British Commonwealth which is usually referred to as Dominion Status. That status, combining as it does all the advantages of unfettered freedom with those of an association of incalculable value both in peace and war, is, I venture to assert, the highest in the world. It is the status of this country and we, at any rate, are not insensible either of the practical advantages or of the honour of our position. It went on, in the very spirit of the Atlantic Charter, to make it clear that we wished India to enjoy that position under a Constitution framed primarily by Indians, for Indians, in accordance with Indian conceptions. We added that while the completion of that undertaking obviously could not take place in the middle of a life and death struggle we were ready to welcome and promote any steps representative Indians might take now to come together and prepare the ground, and that we agreed to the setting up with the least possible delay, after the war, of a body representative of the principal elements of India's national life, and pledged ourselves to lend every aid in our power to hasten decisions on all relevant matters. So far as we are concerned we have offered the utmost expedition in bringing about a constitutional settlement after the war. The actual time-table is, in the main, in the hands of Indians themselves.

Ah! But I shall be told that all this is limited and circumscribed by saying that it is 'subject to the due fulfilment of the obligations which Great Britain's long connexion with India has imposed upon her'. But would any one suggest that the framing of any new form of government in pursuance of the Atlantic Charter could take place anywhere without provision for the fulfilment of pre-existing obligations? What after all are those obligations? They fall into certain main categories—I am not of course giving an exhaustive list. There are, for instance, the actual contractual obligations to the existing members of the services, which naturally expire in due course. Is it suggested that the fulfilment of these is an impairment of freedom? There are obligations of the Crown towards the Indian States, except in so far as and to the extent to which they may have joined an Indian Federation. Here again the continuance of similar obligations has been no detraction from self-government whether in Canada, in Australia, or in South Africa.

Of a somewhat different character is the continuing responsibility of His Majesty's Government for the defence of India until India is in a position to take over that burden unaided. So long as the defence of India requires the permanent presence—as distinguished from help in a great emergency—of British forces it is obvious that the Government which provides those forces is entitled to retain a measure of control over their employment in peace as well as over the external policy which may call for their employment in war. That is not a derogation of status, but a concession to the facts of a particular situation. That situation will be modified, on the one hand by the growth of India's own military resources—and they are growing day by day. It may be modified also by changes in the nature of the possible dangers which may confront India after the war. The precise adjustment of these matters is clearly one that must depend on the circumstances of the immediate post-war situation and on its subsequent development. It need in no way prejudice or delay the establishment in India of a system of government framed by Indians for themselves or the recognition of the equality of that government with the other free governments of the Commonwealth.

How, then, are Indians to frame a system of government for India? How, I might ask, has it been found possible elsewhere to frame a scheme of free self-government, not for a comparatively small and homogeneous people, but for a complex of races, interests and political units which have nevertheless recognized the need of a wider constitutional framework as essential to their security, or their economic welfare, or to the expression of an underlying national sentiment? The answer is that it has never been possible except on the basis of free negotiation, compromise, and eventual agreement between the main elements concerned. It has been so in the case of every British Dominion. In Canada and South Africa the elements to be reconciled were racial as well as local. No American, I imagine, who thinks of the way in which the American Union came about would imagine that in the application of the Atlantic Charter to India any other method could solve the problem. That at any rate has been the view of His Majesty's Government who have made it clear that the future Constitution of India must be framed by agreement between representatives of the principal elements in her national life and refused to contemplate the transfer of their present responsibilities for the peace and welfare of India to any system of government whose authority is directly denied by large and powerful elements in that national life.

What are these principal elements in India's national life? They are first of all the political units into which India is already divided. There are the eleven Provinces of British India—Bengal with a population larger than that of the United Kingdom, Madras with an area as large as Italy—enjoying already or at any rate in a position to enjoy, a wide extent of self-government. There are the States, equally excluded from the control of India's general foreign, defence, and economic policy, but with no similarly precise demarcation between their powers and those of the Crown. There are, secondly, the great religious and cultural communities, above all the two main ones, Hinduism and Islam, with a third, that of the so-called Scheduled Castes, numbering, perhaps, forty millions or more, but unorganized and only gradually acquiring a collective consciousness. Fortunately, from the point of view of a solution of the problem of the Central Constitution, the Moslems, though less than a third of the population of British India, are not a minority everywhere. They are in fact a majority in four out of the eleven Provinces. It should therefore be possible for them in large measure to safeguard their interests by provisions clearly defining the rights of the units. Their outlook is likely, to that extent at any rate, to coincide with that of the States.

You may ask what is meant by agreement ? Does it mean that the attainment of full Indian self-government can be indefinitely held up by the veto of some extreme section on some issue of detail ? Obviously not. It means substantial agreement by the main elements on the main principles of the Constitution. I do not believe that if agreement on those main principles is once reached the details will present an insuperable difficulty in India any more than elsewhere. Nor can I bring myself to believe that there is among Indian statesmen so little constitutional capacity, so little genuine Indian patriotism or, for that matter, so little real desire to see India governed by Indians that they would prefer to disagree indefinitely rather than work out some solution reasonably acceptable all round. It would be inconsistent with the assumption upon which the whole of our policy is based, the assumption of India's fitness for Dominion status, to accept the view that Indians are incapable of agreeing at any rate upon the basis of a Constitution. For if they are incapable of that moral and intellectual effort how are they likely to be capable of the no less great effort of working any Constitution that might be imposed on them ?

This insistence upon the necessity of agreement rules out, of course, any Constitution decided by a mere majority vote. Nor has the principle of a majority vote, applicable as it is to the decision of day by day issues under an accepted Constitution, ever been regarded as applicable either to the framing of a Constitution embracing varied elements or even to its modification. It is this issue, more than any other, which underlies the vehement opposition of the Congress Party to the policy laid down by His Majesty's Government and acceptable, in general principle, to the other elements which make up India's national life. What Congress has demanded is that India's future Constitution should be settled by a Constituent Assembly elected by universal adult suffrage over the whole of India. It is an impossible demand, and yet a natural and intelligible one. It is not merely that Congress, as by far the best organized political machine, would hope to sweep most of the Hindu constituencies. It is more than that. Congress originated and grew up as the first vigorous expression of Indian national ideals in a unified bureaucratic India. It has tended throughout to think of itself as the representative of India in opposition to alien rule, and as the natural heir and successor to that rule. In so doing it is apt to forget that the conditions under which it has grown, under which it has secured its majorities, and under which those majorities have exercised power, will no longer be present if British control and the support of British armed force are removed. It has yet to learn that the conditions under which it can exercise its influence, and fulfil its ideals, in a self-governing India, have yet to be agreed with other elements which are not prepared to consider Congress majorities as having moral authority over them or any other material sanction than that of the existing British authorities.

The difficulty extends not only to the method of finding a Constitution, but to the character of the Constitution itself. Here again the Congress leaders have quite naturally imbibed, not only British democratic ideals, but British ideas as to the best type of democratic Constitution. Nor have we, for our part, ever encouraged India to think in any other terms than those familiar to us, of a Constitution under which the Executive is directly responsible to a party majority in the legislature. What we—and most Indian politicians in the past—have overlooked is that our type of Constitution can only work in a relatively homogeneous community in which parties are the machinery for the expression of differences of views on specific public issues, the nuclei round which the main fluctuating mass of the electorate forms and reforms itself, but embody no permanent differences either of way of life or of underlying loyalties. Unfortunately these conditions do not exist in India, at any rate in the India of today. That is why the All-India Federal Constitution of 1935, devised with such infinite care and forethought, has failed to command support. Rightly or wrongly the experience of Provincial self-government on British Parliamentary lines has convinced the Moslems and the States that they cannot submit to any central government for India in which the Executive is directly dependent upon a parliamentary majority which, if Provincial experience is any guide, would only be the obedient mouthpiece of the Congress High Command.

The inherent difficulties in the way of a federation on British parliamentary lines are not, of course, in themselves obstacles either to federalism or to democracy. Free government has many forms and we should be the last to proclaim a sealed pattern for liberty. I am not going to suggest to you any particular direction in which an alternative solution can best be sought. That is precisely the task which we have invited Indians to undertake for themselves in accordance with their own conceptions and their own conditions, and for which they are clearly best fitted. Moreover it is in the process of coming to an agreement on their future Constitution that Indian statesmen will be in the best position and in the best mood to work it satisfactorily. No Constitution is likely to work when imposed on those who do not believe in it. No doubt India may be able to look for precedents in many directions. Switzerland, the United States, the old German Empire, the former Austro-Hungary—there have been many composite structures outside the British Commonwealth, as well as those of the Commonwealth itself, which may afford helpful precedents or suggestions. Nor is there any reason why Indian political genius should not create precedents of its own. The whole field of policy is open to them, and while they will naturally build, wherever they can, on what exists and what they have been accustomed to work, there are no arbitrary limits imposed on their free choice.

The task before Indian statesmanship is no doubt immensely difficult. But it is certainly not hopeless. Beneath all the differences of religion, of culture, of race and political structure, there is an underlying unity. There is the fundamental geographical unity which has walled India off from the outside world while, at the same time, erecting no serious internal barriers. There is the broad unity of race which makes Indians as a whole, whatever their differences among themselves, a distinctive type among the main races of mankind. There is the political unity which she has enjoyed from time to time in her history, and which we have confirmed in far stronger fashion than any of our predecessors in a unity of administration, of law, of economic development and of communications. I would say, indeed, that if some sort of Indian unity had not existed it would have to be invented. If India were broken up and reverted to chaos tomorrow, Indians would have to set about trying to invent for her at any rate some minimum of unity against the dangers from outside. Why then should they not take her over now as a going concern, though one remoulded nearer to their own heart's desire ?

I have purposely avoided dwelling on the immediate features of the Indian problem for the very reason that they are only the outcome of underlying difficulties, and of that reluctance to abandon accustomed methods of thought in order to solve those difficulties of which I have been speaking. It is the recognition of those difficulties which alone can solve the present deadlock. Recognition, I mean, by Indians, for until there is that recognition there can be no permanent solution. Meanwhile there is no immediate solution that we can bring, for the simple reason that there is no temporary interim step forward which does not run the risk of prejudging, at any rate in Indian eyes, the ultimate solution. That was why Congress would not look last year at the proposed extension of the Viceroy's Executive by the inclusion of political leaders though we endeavoured to do so on lines which, in our opinion at any rate, could not in any way have prejudged the future settlement. That was why Mr Jinnah, the leader of the Moslem League, while regarding our general declaration of policy as satisfactory, was only prepared to join the Viceroy's Council on terms that would have prejudged the future in another sense, and has since then refused to allow members of his League even to join so purely advisory a body as the new National Defence Council, concerned though it is merely with the war effort. The most that we have been able to do has been to bring into the centre of government within the existing Constitution a number of individual Indian statesmen of experience and reputation outside the ordinary party machines who have been prepared to serve India and to increase the efficiency of her war effort. That step, which has converted the Viceroy's Executive from one predominantly British to one predominantly Indian, has not affected the letter of the Indian Constitution. But it has involved a modification in its spirit, the actual effect of which can only be judged in course of time.

Meanwhile the Indian Army has won distinction for itself in many hard-fought fields. The Indian soldier has shown a remarkable aptitude for modern mechanized warfare. The young Indian officers, the product of India's Military Academy, have shown gifts of leadership in junior command which go far to justify the hope that they will grow in due course to the exercise of leadership in the highest ranks. The equipment of India's armies is today, to an extent little dreamt of in the last war, based on India's own industrial capacity. In a very real sense India is today the main arsenal of the Eastern theatre of war. These are matters not directly affecting the structure of a Constitution but most assuredly affecting its essentials. Political status, whether described as Dominion status or otherwise, is a thing which is not conferred like a decoration, but is acquired by the power to exercise and defend it, and in the world of today that power is more necessary than ever before. That power in its turn can only be effectively sustained in the long run by the general vigour, physical and intellectual, of the national life. The problems of nutrition and education are, indeed, in many ways the greatest problems which India has to solve and their solution will be essential to the effective maintenance of whatever constitutional fabric she may devise.

I admit that sometimes when I contemplate the inherent and inexorable difficulties of the Indian problem and still more the unnecessary difficulties of mutual suspicion, mistrust and exaggerated party and communal bias, I feel inclined to wonder whether any individual can really contribute much to the goal which we all would wish to see attained. But then again when I think of what has been achieved in India in the past by ourselves, when I think also of all that India herself has contributed and can yet contribute by her native genius to her own future and, indeed, to the world, when I think of how often in the complex and shifting fabric of history the action of even the least of us, animated by plain good intention, has turned the scale—then I return to my daily task encouraged and sustained, as Burke once bade us to be sustained in dealing with the problem of America, by the ancient motto of the Church, 'Sursum Corda'—'Let us lift up our hearts'.

VI

INDIA'S WAR EFFORT

HOUSE OF COMMONS, NOVEMBER 20TH, 1940

FOR months now our attention has inevitably been absorbed in the contest around and above us and in the immediate problems which it has created. Here and nowhere else the first decisive issue of the war has been fought and won. But if this battle of Britain has closed a chapter it has certainly not closed the story. The actual menace of invasion is still there in the background. We certainly cannot afford to disregard it. At the same time it is becoming increasingly clear that our enemies, foiled in their hope of destroying us by an early fatal blow at the heart, mean to strike directly at every part and, above all, at every vital artery, which they can reach. The battle of Britain is leading up to the battle of the Empire. It is leading up to it in more than one sense. For it is not only on and over fields and seas remote from here that the fate of the world will yet be decided, but it is only by the resources and resolution of a united Empire that ultimate victory can be assured. That is why my right hon. Friend has done well to ask that we should now devote a day to discussion of that part, at any rate, of the Empire's effort for which this House is in the last resort responsible, and I am glad to have this opportunity of telling the House something of the contribution which India and Burma have made and are preparing to make to our common cause.

Before doing so I hope I may be pardoned if I draw the attention of the House to one feature of the situation which has governed and conditioned our effort here and even more in the countries of the Empire. The war of today is essentially a war of machines. The increasingly complex equipment of a modern army cannot be improvised in haste. Even in the most highly industrialized countries months and even years are required to set up the plant with which that equipment can be made. We know what we are suffering here for our well-intentioned unwillingness to realize the greatness of the danger which threatened our freedom and that of the world. If we here are still struggling to make good our deficiencies, our other partners in the Empire have even more leeway to make up because their preparation began even later and because the equipment of their forces has of necessity been postponed to the more urgent demands here where we have had to meet the enemy's first onset.

India played a great part in the last war. Her first divisions brought an invaluable reinforcement to our thin and war-spent front line in France in the autumn of 1914. She bore the whole brunt of the Mesopotamian campaign. Her cavalry played a conspicuous part in Allenby's great cavalry sweep and her infantry exploited it by their amazing march from Jaffa to Alexandretta. In all she put over a million and a half trained men into the field. She can do so again if so many are needed, if once the equipment is there. There is no scarcity of willing recruits. Some 25,000 indeed, of those who have offered themselves, have had to be temporarily relegated. The other day the announcement of 300 vacancies in the Indian Air Force Reserve brought in 18,000 applications. Let me, in passing, emphasize the point that India's fighting forces are all composed of volunteers. There is in force a limited measure of compulsion for Europeans in India and for Indian technical munition workers—in each case not for lack of volunteers but for the sake of fairness and more efficient organization. But the men who are fighting for India are men who have joined of their own free will. There is no shortage of them either in numbers or in quality. But for the moment equipment governs everything and it is upon the equipment situation that the expansion of India's war effort has depended and will continue to depend. I shall come back in a moment to what has been accomplished and what we look forward to accomplishing in that direction. Meanwhile I should like to draw the attention of the House to what India has already achieved or is in process of achieving in regard to the actual expansion of her armed forces.

The Army in India consists in peace time of 160,000 men of the Indian Army and of some 50,000 British troops. The Indian Army is being rapidly expanded, as a first step, to a force of something like 500,000 men of all arms, trained, equipped and mechanized on the modern scale. As a first step over 100,000 recruits have already been taken on of whom a large proportion are by now fully trained. Not the least of the problems of such an expansion is the provision of officers and of training facilities. New officer cadet units both for Indian and for British cadets have been established. There has been a continuous multiplication of schools for advanced training in all branches of military knowledge and in the use of new weapons. The mechanical transport of the Indian Army has been brought up from 5,000 to 32,000 vehicles, a figure which will be doubled next year. Every credit is due to Sir Robert Cassels, the Commander-in-Chief and to his staff, as well as to the Viceroy and the members of his Council more directly concerned, Sir Ramaswami Mudaliar and Sir Muhammad Zafrullah Khan, for laying down and getting under way the difficult initial stages of an expansion whose full results will only be seen as the war develops.

Of this force, India's first army, some 60,000 are already serving overseas. From the very beginning India has reinforced and is continuing to reinforce our garrisons in Malaya and Aden and our army in the Middle East. The Indian transport contingent which showed such admirable steadiness and discipline in France is now playing an active part in the defence of this island. Indian troops won well-deserved praise for their gallantry in Somaliland and have recently played a leading part in the operations at Gallabat. Both in the Middle and the Far East these Indian troops are very directly contributing to India's defence. They are securing her bastions both west and east. Meanwhile there is no neglect of the ever-present problem of India's own immediate frontier defence, and as fast as formations are sent overseas new formations are raised to replace them.

No statement about the Indian Army would be complete without a reference either to the military forces of the Indian States or to those of the Kingdom of Nepal. The importance to India of being able to draw freely for recruits upon the splendid military material of Nepal's Gurkha fighting men needs no stress. All I need say is that we can rely with confidence on the help that our old and loyal ally can afford in that direction. As for the ruling Princes of India they have their own great martial tradition and a long record of loyalty to the Imperial Crown. Not only their forces, but they themselves played a worthy part in the last war. I remember so well the meeting at our Corps Headquarters at Merville in November 1914 between Lord Roberts and that splendid old warrior and comrade in arms of his, Sir Partab Singh of Jodhpur. 'Well, old friend, what have you come to do here ?' asked the great little Field Marshal. 'To die, I hope, for my King,' was the simple reply, and if he failed to achieve his wish it was not for want of trying. In the present war the forces of the Indian States are being steadily enlarged and brought to a higher state of efficiency. Some thirty units are serving with His Majesty's Forces in British India and that fine body, the Bikaner Camel Corps, is already in the Middle East. Ruler after ruler has placed his personal service and the resources of his State unreservedly at the disposal of the King-Emperor.

The Indian Air Force was started on a small scale in 1932 after the first batch of Indian cadets had been trained at Cranwell. Schemes for expansion were put into force immediately on the outbreak of war and existing training facilities greatly enlarged. There is great enthusiasm for the Air Service in India, and young Indians, with their quick minds and sensitive hands, take naturally to flying. Not a few Indian pilots are already serving in the Royal Air Force and a batch of keen Indian pilots arrived here only the other day to complete their training. Nothing, indeed, except the imperious limitation imposed by the more urgent demand for machines here and in the Middle East stands in the way of a far greater expansion of India's eagerness to develop an air force comparable to her army. That same inevitable limitation again has hitherto prevented the immediate realization of India's widespread demand for the starting of an effective aircraft industry of her own.

Last but not least, comes the Royal Indian Navy, the lineal descendant of an Indian Naval Service which began as the East India Company's Marine as far back as 1612. Reorganized on a small scale in 1934 it, with its auxiliary services, has been more than trebled since the outbreak of war and is being steadily increased by new vessels in construction in India, in Australia, and in this country. Indefatigably occupied with the task of escorting convoys and keeping India's ports and coasts clear of enemy mines and submarines, the Royal Indian Navy is worthily maintaining the high traditions of its past. The sinking of H.M.I.S. *Pathan* last June by enemy action afforded an occasion for a display of exemplary coolness and discipline on the part of all concerned under peculiarly trying conditions. It is some evidence of the efficiency of its work in co-operation with the Royal Navy that since the outbreak of war a continuous stream of troops and military supply ships have sailed without a single casualty from Indian ports to the Middle East, and that the Red Sea is being kept open for pilgrim traffic to the Moslem Holy Places. A word, too, is due, while I am on the subject of the sea, to the faithful and efficient service of India's merchant mariners, the lascars who form so important a part of the crews of so many of our great shipping lines.

May I now revert to what I made clear at the outset is the dominant factor in the whole situation, the factor of supply and equipment? In this respect India, like the Dominions, is far more advanced than she was in 1914. She has always been a great producer of foodstuffs and raw materials, and her resources in this respect, too, have been greatly developed. But she is also today one of the world's great industrial countries. She has highly developed textile industries in cotton, in jute and in wool. She has an iron and steel industry developing rapidly both in its volume, which now amounts to two and a quarter million tons a year, and in the range of its products. At the present moment, over and above supplying the Middle East, Iraq, and East Africa with steel, she is sending substantial quantities of pig-iron to this country. Her railway works and many of her civil engineering establishments are on a great scale and equipped on modern lines. She has considerable resources of hydro-electric power. Her Government ordnance and munition works had also developed in many directions before the outbreak of war, and have been utilized to the full and greatly expanded since. India already makes her own rifles, machine-guns, field artillery up to six-inch guns and six-inch howitzers, propellents and ammunition of all sorts, as well as saddlery, boots, tents, blankets, uniforms, and miscellaneous equipment of all sorts. Of some 40,000 items which go to the equipment of a modern army she already supplies more than one-half. She is beginning the manufacture of armoured plate and expects to armour 3,000 armoured vehicles next year. In respect of something like 90 per cent. of military supplies she will soon be self-sufficient so far as the requirements of her own forces are concerned. Over a very large range of supplies, indeed, she can furnish far more than her own requirements. To quote only a few instances: she has sent overseas 100,000,000 rounds of small arms ammunition and 400,000 rounds of gun ammunition, 1,000,000,000 sandbags, 1,000,000 pairs of boots, and 30,000 tents. Broadly speaking she is aiming, in co-operation with the Dominions and Colonies east and south of Suez, at meeting, in respect of a very wide and steadily increasing range of the whole field of military equipment, all the needs of our armies in the Middle and Far East to whatever number of divisions they may be raised.

Even so there is still abundant room for the further expansion of India's effort. She still has great reserves of industrial capacity which could be harnessed to war purposes if they could be matched up with a certain modicum of imported materials and with certain types of machine tools and organized on lines which we have worked out here. In order to afford India the benefit of our latest experience in this direction, as well as to furnish the Ministry of Supply here with a revised picture of India's potentialities and of the help required to convert them into actualities, the then Minister of Supply sent out some three months ago, at my suggestion, a strong technical mission under the leadership of Sir Alexander Roger. I believe that with Sir Alexander Roger's drive and vision, and with the eager co-operation both of Government and of private industry in India, the mission will be able to initiate a substantial advance, both in volume and in range of production, the fruits of which will become increasingly apparent as the war continues.

The mere re-organization of plant will not produce results without trained workers. I have already referred to the fact that a limited measure of compulsory service has been introduced by the Government of India in order to enable skilled technical workers to be transferred to where their work will be most valuable. This is being done through Indian National Service Labour tribunals in the interests of fairness as well as efficiency, and with appropriate guarantees for the security of the workers' original employment after the war. In India itself arrangements for training additional skilled workers are being taken in hand on a large scale and it is hoped, by the use of the staffs of technical colleges and institutions as well as with the help of private industry, to train an additional 10,000 men in the next few months. Meanwhile my right hon. Friend the Minister of Labour and myself have been concerting arrangements both for the dispatch to India of an additional supply of competent instructors and for the bringing of young Indian workers over here where, working side by side with British workers, they may learn not only our most up-to-date methods but something of the spirit of British industrial organization as displayed in its co-operation with the war effort.

So much of the material aspect of India's share in the common effort against the common enemy. What of the moral and spiritual side? Where does India stand in the struggle against the forces of tyranny and oppression? Where are her sympathies enlisted, with which side are her interests identified? I shall be dealing later this afternoon with the statement which has just been made by the Viceroy in the Indian Legislature and which is now available as a White Paper as well as with the political issues raised by the attitude of Congress. But on one main issue at any rate there is certainly no divergence among the leaders of Indian opinion, whatever other differences there may be between us or between themselves. They know that the defeat of the British Empire and the victory of the dictatorships would leave India defenceless against inevitable aggression from every quarter by land, by sea, or by air. They know more. They know it would mean the end of all their cherished hopes of constitutional progress within India, and in India's relation to the outside world. For them, as for us, a Nazi victory would be a death blow to all they care for in the world of politics.

One form in which that sympathy has been expressed has been in the contributions which have poured in spontaneously from Indians in every walk of life, from ruling Princes to working men, some giving lakhs of rupees, some only a few annas, both to the Viceroy's general War Purposes Fund, and to every fund raised in the country for purposes connected with the war.

Of the sums given for specific purposes, about £1,500,000—including £290,000 from Hyderabad alone—have been given for the purchase of aircraft. But large amounts have also been contributed to King George's Fund for Sailors, to St. Dunstan's Institute for those blinded in the war, to the Red Cross, for ambulances, for the evacuation of children, and, more recently, to the Lord Mayor's Fund for the victims of air attack here and to the cause of Greece. Many of the letters accompanying small sums involving real sacrifices for their donors give simple but poignant expression to the senders' devotion to the common cause.

From India let me turn for a moment tò the subject of Burma. When the war broke out Burma had been in existence as a separate entity for only about two and a half years. Her defence forces at that time consisted of two British regular infantry battalions and four battalions of the Burma Rifles as well as six battalions of the Burma Frontier Force. Since the outbreak of the war these forces have been very largely increased. A number of other technical units, sappers and miners, signals, transport, anti-aircraft, machine-gun units, &c., have been added since the outbreak of the war. Compulsory service has been introduced for Europeans, both for military purposes and for the general war effort. The reserve of officers has been greatly expanded and arrangements have been completed for the initiation of an Officer Cadet Training Unit in which both Europeans and Burman volunteers will be trained side by side. Here again, as in the case of India, while every effort is being made to modernize the equipment of the forces in Burma, much depends upon the supplies which can be secured from the United Kingdom or from India.

Before the war Burma had no naval or air forces of her own. Immediately on the outbreak of war, however, three local vessels were taken over for mine-sweeping duties and a Burma Royal Naval Volunteer Reserve created. Several naval patrol craft for mine-sweeping are now in process of completion, and the Government of Burma have arranged in consultation with the Admiralty for the building for the Royal Navy of some mine-sweepers and anti-submarine vessels. So far as air force is concerned a Burma Auxiliary Air Unit open to both Burmans and Europeans in Burma has been started, but is as yet only at the initial training stage.

Burma's main productive capacity is, of course, in the direction of raw materials. She is a great producer of oil as well as of valuable minerals like lead, zinc, and wolfram, and of timber and foodstuffs. Her manufacturing capacity, on the other hand, is limited, but her possibilities of munitions production will no doubt be fully considered by the Delhi Conference of which I shall have a word to say in a moment. Meanwhile, Burma, like India, has shown her moral support of the common cause by the readiness in which contributions of every kind have poured in to the war fund. A Burma Fighter Squadron of the R.A.F. has been provided by these funds, which in all, up to date, have amounted to over £210,000. It is interesting to note that £60,000 of this have come from the Shan States, partly from their federal fund and partly from individual chiefs, and that, within their capacity, tribal chiefs from the remote hill districts and municipalities in Upper and Lower Burma have freely offered their contributions of gifts or interest-free loans. In February and again in June, the Legislature and Council of Ministers have made plain their whole-hearted support of the British Government in its stand against the forces of aggression and its struggle for the freedom of small nations.

So far I have spoken of India and Burma as self-contained units. But they do not stand alone. They stand geographically at the centre of that greater half of the British Empire—greater in area and far greater in population—which, from the Cape to New Zealand, lies in a vast semi-circle round the Southern Ocean. Strategically they form the direct first reserve not only against the immediate threat to our position in the Middle East but against any possible threat to our position in the Far East. Between that eastern and southern half of the Empire and this country, the normal highway passes through the Mediterranean and the Suez Canal. At the moment that I took office the Italian threat to that vital link was already obvious—the doubling of that menace by the defection of France followed only a few weeks later. It was clear to me from the outset that in large measure the defence of the Empire east and south of Suez, as well as of the Middle Eastern front itself, would have to rest upon its own resources. It was equally clear that those resources, in manpower, in industry, in raw materials, were immense if they could be effectively combined and matched with each other. I naturally lost no time in communicating my views to the Viceroy, who throughout has shown the keenest interest in all questions affecting India's war effort. I need not tell the House how glad I am in that connexion that Lord Linlithgow has consented, at no small personal inconvenience to carry on the good work he is doing for an additional year. Promptly converting a general conception into a concrete working plan Lord Linlithgow conceived the idea of inviting all the governments concerned to send to a Conference at Delhi representatives of their departments of military supply and equipment. The Viceroy's initiative met at once with an eager response, and for nearly three weeks now the representatives of the Governments of Australia, New Zealand, the Union of South Africa, Rhodesia, and East African Colonies, Palestine, Burma, and Malaya have been conferring with the Government of India and with Sir Alexander Roger's Mission.

Their immediate object is simple if important. It is to see how in co-operation they can contribute, for their own defence and for the common cause, the very maximum of those elements of supply and equipment upon which the expansion of the Empire's armies must depend. In this respect they are, if I may quote from the Prime Minister's inspiring message to the Conference, engaged in calling into being a new world of armed strength to redress the balance of the old. It may well be that Delhi is laying the foundations of that Army of Empire whose first contingents are defending the Middle East today, but which is destined in its ultimate plenitude of power to march in the van of a liberated Europe.

This aspect of the Delhi Conference, important as it is, is not the only one. It is of the very essence of our conception of the British Commonwealth today that it is not of the nature of a solar system with a central sun and satellite planets revolving round it, but of a partnership of free and equal nations girdling the globe. Its activities, the spirit of unity which binds it together, do not reside in any one part or depend upon any central initiative. We are bound together by common ideals and ways of life and thought, and these are enough to secure collective action between any two or more members of the Commonwealth where such action can best further the causes to which we are all dedicated. From India's point of view, too, this is a most significant gathering. It is a conference of the Empire held in India under the presidency of an Indian member of the Viceroy's Executive, Sir Muhammad Zafrullah Khan. That is a fact which is both a practical recognition of India's growing status in the Commonwealth, as well as a contribution to a better understanding and a future closer collaboration between India and her British neighbours in the Southern hemisphere. Last but not least its outcome is destined to be that growth in India's ability to provide her own defence, and that enrichment of her productive power, which are the real sources of a true independence, and which will do more than anything else to strengthen her claim to that full and equal partnership for mutual security and mutual welfare to which we in this House wish to see her attain.

VII

THE BEVIN BOYS

LETCHWORTH, JUNE 19TH, 1941

YOU have already been welcomed on your arrival by Mr Bevin, the Minister of Labour. Your coming here has been due to his inspiration and enthusiasm and it is under his guidance and direction that your training will be carried out. He has already welcomed you on behalf of the British Government. I have come to welcome you on behalf of the Government of India and to express the hope that you will find both profit and pleasure in your course of training here. You have come to the oldest and most highly developed centre of engineering skill in the world in order to acquire for yourselves and to take back for the benefit of your fellow workers in India all that you can learn from our methods in British industries. The result of your training will, I hope, be of advantage to each one of you, enabling you to earn better money when you get back to India and to make a successful career in your native home. But the object of your coming here is something more than that. It is that you should serve your country, India. At this moment India, in common with ourselves and all the other members of our British Commonwealth, is engaged in battle against the evil forces of aggression, of tyranny, of racial intolerance which are seeking to destroy the world, and which, if victorious, would destroy not only what India enjoys today of ordered freedom but all her hopes for the future. In that battle Indian fighting men in every Service have already taken a memorable part and added fresh glory to India's historic fighting tradition. In modern war, however, everything depends upon the possession of modern equipment, and even the bravest, as Poland and France and Yugoslavia have shown, are helpless against overwhelming superiority in machines.

Today the men who make the instruments of war are no less essential a part of the battle than the men who fight in the actual front line, and here, in England, at any rate, you will find that they are also exposed to many of the same dangers. If India is to play her part worthily in this war it is not enough that she should find, as she is doing, hundreds of thousands of splendid, willing recruits. She must also make the weapons without which they cannot overcome their enemies. That is the great task upon which India is entering today and for the fulfilment of that task she needs more trained and skilled technical workers. That is the part of India's battle which you are undertaking, both by what you can learn here for yourselves and by what you can teach others when you return to India.

You have come to serve your country in the present struggle. But you will also serve her hereafter. India can never be fully prosperous or strong enough to maintain a free national life until she has developed her industrial as well as her agricultural resources. You will be helping to build up that future as well.

There are other things you may be able to learn here as well as technical skill. This country is the original home of Trade Unionism and it is here that industrial organization on the part of working men has reached its fullest development. If you have opportunities of studying that organization here you will discover how soundly based it is and with what sense of responsibility its leaders work, not in quarrel and strife with capital, but in fruitful partnership with it to maintain reasonable standards both of remuneration and of conditions of work for all employed in industry. Such free association, used for particular purposes, but also with regard to the common national interest—above all in a time of national danger like the present—is a characteristic feature of the life of this country. It is something the German workmen endeavoured to imitate but which has been ruthlessly stamped out by Nazi tyranny.

Your long journey and your stay here together may also teach you something that you may not have expected to learn, namely, something about India. You come from different parts of India and belong to different communities and while at home may have thought little about India as a whole. During your voyage here and still more among a different people you may have become much more conscious of the fact that underlying your minor differences you are all Indians and belong to India. That is something you should feel proud of, proud of India's wonderful past and of the greater future that is in store for her, eager to do credit to India while you are here and to do something for India when you return. Some of you may take part in public affairs later on and I can only hope that the result of your visit here may have strengthened your loyalty to India and will make you put India first, above all local and communal differences, in what you say and do in public life.

Lastly, you will, by the time you leave, have learnt something about this country and its people. They are, I believe, the most civilized people in this world and by that I mean most understanding in the art of living and working together freely. You will also I think learn that the kindliness and tolerance of this people, and its deep love of peace, have not deprived them of courage in facing whatever dangers this struggle may bring to them. You will, I hope, return, not only with happy individual experiences of the men and women you will have met and the homes where you have stayed, but also with an understanding of this country and with the belief that India can choose no better future in this difficult world than continuing to work in partnership with us, not only for safety in war, but also for the progress and welfare of each by mutual co-operation in peace.

VIII

THE DECLARATION OF AUGUST 1940

HOUSE OF COMMONS, AUGUST 14TH, 1940

I HOPE that I may claim the indulgence of the House, not only because this is the first time, after a long interval of years, that I speak from this Box, but because of the importance and difficulty of the subject with which I have to deal. To keep one's balance steadily along a knife-edge of ice in the high Alps is a much easier task than threading one's way, without stumbling or offence, through the intricate, pitfall-strewn maze of the present Indian situation. So I trust that before hon. Members enter upon a discussion of the important statement made by the Viceroy last week, they will bear patiently with me while I endeavour to say something about the background of political controversy and deadlock which led up to that statement. It is only in that way that the full significance and purport of Lord Linlithgow's initiative and the decision of His Majesty's Government in this matter can be rightly understood.[1]

Five years have passed since the passage of the Government of India Act. That Measure was the fruit of a long series of commissions and conferences and many stirring Debates in this House. It was, in itself, a remarkable feat of constructive statesmanship on the part of Parliament and, so far as the Provincial part of the Act is concerned, it presently came into operation and is still being worked successfully in four out of eleven Provinces of India. If it is temporarily suspended in the other Provinces, that fact has not been due to any failure on the part of the Provincial Ministries to carry out the responsibilities entrusted to them, or to any conflict between them and the Provincial Governors or the Central Government; but to purely extraneous

[1] See Appendix I.

causes of which I shall have something to say in a moment. Whether the Federal provisions of the Act might have worked equally well, if they could have been brought into operation promptly is, perhaps, an open question. What is certain is that the delays involved, inevitable as they may have been, have afforded occasion for the development of a volume of adverse criticism and of opposition, in face of which their enforcement could no longer serve the purpose for which they were originally devised. It is essential to keep in mind that this opposition comes from different quarters, and indeed, is based on opposite reasons. The constitutional deadlock in India today is not so much between His Majesty's Government and a consentient Indian Opposition, as between the main elements in India's own national life. It can therefore not be resolved by the relatively easy method of bilateral agreement between His Majesty's Government and the representatives of India but only by the much more difficult method of multi-lateral agreement, in which His Majesty's Government is only one of the parties concerned.

Let me say a word about this problem. There is, first of all, the Indian National Congress. Its leaders repudiate the Act of 1935, at any rate in its Federal aspect, as a denial both of India's right to immediate complete independence and of the principles of democracy. It was in pursuance of that repudiation, and because India's consent was not formally invited before she was committed to war that they called out the Congress Ministries in the Provinces. Their demand has been that India's independence should be recognized forthwith, and that Indians should devise their own Constitution in a Constituent Assembly elected by universal adult suffrage over all India, including the Indian States. In the last few weeks they have declared their willingness in the meantime to join in the war effort through a National Government commanding the confidence of the elected members of the Legislative Assembly.

The Congress leaders are men animated and inspired by an ardent national patriotism. They have built up a remarkable political organization, by far the most efficient political machine in India, of which they are justly proud. They have striven to make that organization national and all-embracing. If only they had succeeded, if Congress could, in fact, speak as it professes to speak, for all the main elements in India's national life, then, however advanced their demands, our problem might have been very different and in many respects far easier than it is today. It is true that they are numerically much the largest single party in British India. But their claim, in virtue of that fact, to speak for India, is utterly denied by very important elements in India's complex national life. These other elements assert their right to be regarded, not as mere numerical minorities, but as separate constituent factors in any future Indian polity, entitled to be treated as such in any discussions for the shaping of India's future Constitution.

Foremost among these elements stands the great Moslem community, 90,000,000 strong, and constituting a majority both in north-western and north-eastern India, but scattered as a minority over the whole sub-continent. In religious and social outlook, in historic tradition and culture, the difference between them and their Hindu fellow countrymen goes as deep as, if not deeper than, any similar or corresponding difference in Europe. That need not and does not preclude pleasant social intercourse or fruitful political co-operation. It has not, in fact, prevented individual Moslems taking an active part in the work of the Congress Party. But as a body the Moslems have stood aloof. Their quarrel with the scheme of the existing Act is not that it fails to give that clear majority rule for which Congress asks, but that, on the contrary, it gives too great powers to a Hindu majority at the Centre. They will have nothing to do with a Constitution framed by a Constituent Assembly elected by majority vote in geographical constituencies. They claim the right in any constitutional discussions to be regarded as an entity and are determined only to accept a Constitution whose actual structure will secure their position as an entity against the operation of a mere numerical majority. The same, though in a lesser degree perhaps, applies to the great body of what are known as the Scheduled Castes, who feel, in spite of Mr Gandhi's earnest efforts on their behalf, that, as a community, they stand outside the main body of the Hindu community which is represented by Congress.

The Indian Princes, again, with territories which cover a third of all India, and which include nearly a quarter of its population, constitute another entity or group of entities which refuses to be assimilated to the simple democratic formula propounded by Congress. They object to the existing scheme as interfering too greatly with their existing powers. They naturally object even more strongly to the proposed Constituent Assembly or any Constitution which might emerge from it. Yet they are an essential element in any Indian Federation. What is more, they can make a most valuable contribution to it. In many ways their territories are the most characteristically Indian part of India. They have equally much to gain from closer contact with the rest of India in constitutional as well as in economic development. But it is idle to suppose that such a development can take place overnight or that it can be forced upon them before they can be allowed to play their part in a federal scheme. It is essential to keep these differences in mind when we talk of finding a solution for India's constitutional problem. They are, at the moment, still unbridged. I refuse to regard them as unbridgeable. Underlying them, after all, there is the fact that India is a self-contained and distinctive region of the world. There is the fact that India can boast of an ancient civilization and of a long history common to all her peoples, of which all Indians are equally proud. Is there any Indian who is not proud to be called an Indian ? Is there any Indian, of any community, who has not felt a thrill of pride in the thought that he is a fellow countryman of a man like Rabindranath Tagore, who was so uniquely honoured by Oxford University the other day ? Underlying them, too, is another unity, a unity not merely of administration, but of political thought and aspiration which we here can justly claim to have contributed to India's national life. India cannot be unitary in the sense that we, in this island, are unitary, but she can still be a unity. India's future house of freedom has room for many mansions.

In no respect has the essential unity of India's outlook been shown more clearly than in the attitude which all parties and communities have from the outset of this war taken up in their detestation of Nazi aggression and in their endorsement of our common cause. The greater our difficulties, the graver the disasters that befell the Allied arms, the clearer has been the realization in the minds of the Indian public that our cause is India's cause, the stronger the wave of sympathetic emotion for this country in its single-handed fight, the more widespread has been the feeling that a purely political deadlock, affecting the issues of today and to-morrow, ought not to be allowed to stand in the way of India's contributing a united and whole-hearted effort to the cause upon whose victory depends the preservation of all her ideals and the fulfilment of all her aspirations. It is in this atmosphere that the Viceroy felt that the moment had come for an initiative which should at the same time enlist all the elements of political leadership in India behind her war effort, and also make, at any rate, a beginning in breaking down the existing political deadlock, and so pave the way towards the early achievement of that goal of free and equal partnership in the British Commonwealth which, to quote the eloquent closing words of his statement, is

> 'the proclaimed and accepted goal of the Imperial Crown and of the British Parliament'.

The immediate offer contained in the Viceroy's statement is that of an expansion of his Executive Council as Governor-General, so as to include in it leading members of all political parties, as well as the establishment of a wider War Advisory Council on an all-India basis, associating with the conduct of the war representatives of the Indian States and of other interests in the national life of India as a whole. The enlarged Executive

Council will, of course, under the existing Constitution, still be responsible to the Governor-General, and cannot be responsible in the strict constitutional sense to the Legislature. The Congress have asked that a provisional National Government should be set up at the Centre, which, though formed as a transitory measure, should be such as to command the confidence of all the elected elements in the Central Legislature. In inviting a certain number of representative Indians to join this Council, the Viceroy will naturally take appropriate steps to ensure that the new members do in fact represent the opinion of the parties from which they are chosen. If, however, the Congress claim is that the members of the Viceroy's Council should be dependent on the support of the elected members of the Legislature, it is, in fact, a demand for changing the whole basis of the Government of India in the middle of the war. More than that, if the House has followed the analysis which I have attempted to give of the attitude of the different elements in India to the constitutional problem, it will realize that it is a demand which raises the whole unresolved constitutional issue and prejudges it in the sense favoured by Congress and rejected by the minorities. There can be no agreement on a Government responsible to the Legislature until there is agreement on the nature of the Legislature, and upon the whole structure of the Constitution.

The Congress demand, therefore, in present circumstances is not a practical demand. The Viceroy's offer, on the other hand, does present to Indian leaders the opportunity of taking an immediate, effective, and important part in the government of India and of bringing their influence to bear on the conduct of the war without prejudice to their several political positions. They will commit themselves to nothing, except to working together in the present emergency for the safety and good of India and for the common cause in which they all believe. I still hope that they will be willing to take their part, in spite of the discouraging attitude shown in Congress quarters. If it should, unfortunately, not prove to be the case, Lord Linlithgow will, of course, still go ahead, prepared to work with those who will work with him and with each other.

The Viceroy's immediate offer, however, does not stand by itself. His initiative has been concerned, as I said just now, not only with India's fuller participation in the actual present war effort, but also with paving the way towards the speedier attainment of the goal at which we are aiming. May I say a word about that goal—Dominion status, as it is commonly described, or, as I prefer to describe it, free and equal partnership in the British Commonwealth? It is not, as is so often suggested when Dominion status is contrasted with full independence, an inferior or dependent status. The status of a Dominion—or of this country, for that matter, for our status in the Commonwealth, although not, perhaps, our stature, is the same as theirs—is one not inferior to that of nations that perforce stand alone, but superior. How many so-called independent nations are really free to live their own lives as they will, even when they are not directly overrun or dismembered by more powerful neighbours? We of the British Commonwealth enjoy something more. We enjoy the security, the prosperity, the friendship, the enhanced dignity in the eyes of the world, which come to each of us as the result of our free and equal association. There is no higher status in the world than that. That is the status which we have declared to be the goal of our policy in India.

Our declarations, however, have apparently still left in certain quarters doubts as to the sincerity of our purpose, and have raised, not unnaturally, the question both of the time when and the method by which we mean to fulfil them. It is to that question that the Viceroy, with the full approval of His Majesty's Government, has now given an answer, which marks, I think, a notable step forward on the path to the accepted goal. May I quote here the most significant passage in the Viceroy's statement?

> 'There has been very strong insistence that the framing of that scheme'—that is, the new constitutional scheme for India—'should be primarily the

responsibility of Indians themselves, and should originate from Indian conceptions of the social, economic, and political structure of Indian life. His Majesty's Government are in sympathy with that desire, and wish to see it given the fullest practical expression subject to the due fulfilment of the obligations which Great Britain's long connexion with India has imposed on her and for which His Majesty's Government cannot divest themselves of responsibility.'

The recognition of these obligations is not an impairment of status, but only a recognition of facts, historic or geographical, which differentiate the present position of India from that of other Dominions. As the late Lord Balfour pointed out in his remarkable exposition of the nature of British Commonwealth relations, in the constitutional report of the Imperial Conference of 1926:

'The principles of equality and similarity appropriate to status do not universally extend to function.'

and he instanced, in particular, the functions of defence and foreign policy. It is in respect of these, for example, that the position of India, both in virtue of her historic military organization and of her geographical position, differs from that of the Dominions. But the difference that arises from these and similar obligations is one of degree, and not of kind. For in the case of every Dominion there has always been some measure of adjustment, formal or informal, to British obligations. Subject to these matters, the desire of His Majesty's Government is that the new Constitution of India should be devised by Indians for themselves, and should—may I quote the words again ?—

'originate from Indian conceptions of the social, economic, and political structure of Indian life'.

That task is to be undertaken with the least possible delay after the war by

'a body representative of the principal elements in India's national life'.

That means a body constituted in agreement between the representatives of these elements. It does not mean a body set up on lines which may commend themselves to one particular element, however influential, but wholly unacceptable to the minority elements. His Majesty's Government have made it clear that they could not contemplate the transfer of their present responsibilities for the peace and welfare of India to any system of government whose authority is directly denied by large and powerful elements in India's national life. In this matter too, there is no departure from the principles which have governed the coming into existence of every Dominion Constitution. In every case in the Dominions there has been antecedent agreement, not only between the geographical units, but also between the main racial elements—English and French in Canada, Britain and Boer in South Africa—both as to the method of framing the Constitution and as to the Constitution itself. Agreement, consent, is, indeed, the foundation of all free government, of all true democracy. Decision by majority is not so much of the essence of democracy as a practical convenience, which presupposes for its proper working an antecedent general consent to the Constitution itself. It has, indeed, in most federal Constitutions been limited in various ways in order to safeguard the separate interests of the federating elements. To describe the need for such agreement as a veto on constitutional progress is, I think, to do an injustice to the patriotism and sense of responsibility of those concerned. Agreement means no veto by any element, but compromise. And willingness to compromise, in India as elsewhere, is an essential test of that sense of responsibility on which free government must be based.

On the other hand, within the limitations imposed by the necessity of securing agreement, the whole constitutional field is open to re-examination. It may, indeed, prove to be the case that it is by entirely novel departures from the existing scheme, whether in the relation of the Centre to the Provinces or to the States, or in the methods of election and representation, that an agreement can be reached which is unattainable within the framework of the existing Act, based as it is on the traditions of India's administrative past and on our customary British constitutional conceptions.

So much for the question of method. There is the question, no less insistently asked, as to the date. Here the answer given by the statement is also clear. The decisive resolution of these great constitutional issues, the actual setting up of a new system of government, cannot come at the moment when we are all engaged in a desperate struggle for existence. How soon it can come after the war is essentially in India's own hands. The experience of every Dominion has shown that these fundamental issues are not lightly or speedily settled. What I have told the House of the complexity and difficulty of India's peculiar problems does not suggest that her experience in this respect will be essentially different from that of others. There is always an immense amount of preliminary discussion, inquiry, and negotiation which has to be got through before the real decisive meetings take place. There is absolutely no reason why any of this indispensable preliminary work should wait for the end of the war. The more completely and thoroughly it is done now, the wider the agreement reached now as to the form of the post-war representative body, as to the methods and procedure by which we should arrive at its conclusions, and as to the principles and outlines of the Constitution itself, the more speedily can everything be settled after the war is over. So far as His Majesty's Government are concerned, they have offered to welcome and promote in any way possible such preliminary friendly discussion and investigation and have equally promised to lend every aid in their power to hasten decisions on all relevant matters when it comes to the subsequent task of finally settling the Constitution. They can do no more. The responsibility for securing a speedy as well as a satisfactory result rests upon Indians themselves.

I submit that the Viceroy's initiative represents a sincere effort on our part to make such contribution as we can towards the smooth and speedy attainment of the desired goal. Others must also make their contribution. No one element or party can hope to get all that it wants, or at least to get all at once. If we agree upon the end, let us all work for it with sympathy, understanding, patience, good will towards each other. That, at any rate, is the spirit in which His Majesty's Government are resolved to persevere in the carrying out of the policy which they have now defined. So far as we in this country are concerned, we have every reason to be proud of what we have contributed in the past to the history and to the life of India. But I, at any rate, believe with Lord Macaulay that the proudest day of our history will be the day when we see India joining, a free and willing partner, in the brotherhood of the British peoples. As for India, she will give, I know, her effective answer to tyranny and aggression in the field of war. But she can give an even more conclusive answer in the field of constructive statesmanship. In a world threatened by all the evil forces of hatred and destruction, of partisan and racial intolerance, there could be no more hopeful portent, no more assured omen of the ultimate victory of our cause, than that the leaders of India's millions should in peaceful agreement resolve not only their own perplexing discord, but also afford yet one further example within our British Commonwealth of the power of good will to reconcile freedom and unity, and through our Commonwealth to bridge the age-long gulf between Europe and Asia. Then, indeed, could we say with justice that the dawn of a better day for the world was heralded in the East.

IX

THE PROVINCES AND THE CONSTITUTION

HOUSE OF COMMONS, APRIL 22ND, 1941

THE purpose of the resolutions which I am submitting to the House today is to extend for another twelve months the proclamations issued under the provisions of Section 93 of the India Act. Under the terms of that Section the Governor of a Province, if satisfied that a situation has arisen in which parliamentary government cannot be carried on in accordance with the Act, can by proclamation assume all or any of the powers vested in the provincial bodies and authorities. This situation arose in October, 1939, in consequence of the action of the Congress Party's 'High Command' in ordering the Congress Ministries to resign. Proclamations under Section 93 were accordingly issued in seven provinces, and their continuance in force for a further twelve months was duly approved by the House on April 18th of last year. There has been no change in the situation since then, and we have, I regret to say, no alternative to a further extension of these emergency provisions.

I would remind the House, however, that these resolutions are only concerned with seven out of the eleven provinces of British India. In the four provinces of Bengal, Assam, Sind, and the Punjab, with a population of something like 100 million people—one third of the whole population of British India—provincial self-government has continued to work uninterruptedly under composite Governments, including Moslem and Hindu Ministers. On all the questions which most nearly affect the ordinary life of the citizen—all the questions, in fact, which occupy most of the attention of this House in times of peace—these 100 million of Indians have now for four years been enjoying the advantages of democratic self-government. Ministers and legislators have continued to gain experience and are making their effective contribution, not only to the welfare of their constituents within the wide sphere of their direct authority, but to India's general war effort. We ought not to underestimate the significance of this remarkable advance in self-government over so large a field. Nor can we afford to ignore the importance of the voice which these Provinces, through their governments, are bound to exercise in any deliberations affecting the future Constitution of India.

From this point of view it is a matter of deep regret that the 200 million inhabitants of the other seven Provinces were, by the ukase of the Congress High Command, forbidden to continue to build up the practice and tradition of self-government. Their governments, too, had made a satisfactory beginning, and if they made mistakes—as even we here have been known to do—the remedy lay with their electors. So far, indeed, as the provincial electorates are concerned it must be admitted that they nowhere showed any signs of distress at the suspension of parliamentary government—in this respect, no doubt, differing greatly from what would be the attitude of our own electors if deprived of the services of this front bench. The change to direct personal government by Governors and permanent officials met with general acquiescence and, indeed, good will. Whatever political unrest there may be in India today has certainly not arisen in any way from the suspension of provincial self-government. There has been no discontinuity or abrupt reversal in either administrative or legislative policy. In some instances, indeed, notably in connexion with prohibition, legislation has had to be modified in consequence of legal decisions. But, generally speaking, the work of beneficent social policy continues in full progress and with broad public approval. The House need not therefore fear that the continuance of direct government in these provinces for another twelve months will of itself add to the difficulties of the political situation.

What, indeed, was really serious in the action of the Congress-controlled Ministries was not so much the direct and immediate result of their action in the provinces themselves, as the complete disregard displayed by the most powerful Indian party for the responsibilities of self-government, and the indirect effect of this evidence of Congress methods upon the general political situation. When we speak of responsible parliamentary government we are apt to emphasize one aspect of that responsibility, namely responsibility towards the party majority in the legislature. But responsible parliamentary government, if it is to succeed, implies a threefold responsibility. There is, first and foremost, responsibility to the Crown, in other words to the general welfare, the duty of maintaining the substantial continuity and efficiency of government, of seeing, in the old phrase, that 'the King's Government is carried on'. There is, secondly, the responsibility to Parliament as an institution, founded, if I may say so, Mr Speaker, upon your authority and upon the rights of minorities which, subject to the established procedure of Parliament, are in your keeping. It is only in the third place, and subject to these dominating responsibilities, that a government is responsible to its supporters in Parliament for the promotion of particular policies in which they are interested.

In the present case Ministers resigned, not as the result of any difference with their Governors, not over any issue of provincial policy, not at the instance of their own supporters in Parliament. They resigned, prepared to bring about the complete breakdown of the administrative and parliamentary life of their provinces, at the orders of an outside executive which wished, in this imperious and irresponsible fashion, to express its disapproval of the absence of a statement of war aims by the British Government framed to its liking. I can only say, whatever may have been the motives which inspired the conduct both of the Congress High Command and of the provincial Ministries, that there is no greater danger to democratic government, in India, as elsewhere, than party totalitarianism.

More immediately serious has been the effect of this demonstration of Congress methods upon other important elements in India, the Princes, the non-Congress Provinces, and the Moslem community generally. It has confirmed, to the point of a fixed determination, their already growing reluctance to take part in, or come under, any Central Government in India which is likely to be subject to the control of a majority in the legislature which, in its turn, would obey the orders of the Congress Central Executive. Congress repudiated the Federal provisions of the Act of 1935 largely because they weighted representation in the Legislature, in favour of the minority element, in what it regarded an undemocratic sense. It is, I fear, blind to the risk that no alternative Constitution is now likely to emerge which could secure for it as great a measure of influence and control over India as a whole as it would have exercised under the present Act.

The most significant symptom of the changed situation is the growing strength of the demand, voiced by Mr Jinnah, the leader of the Moslem League, for the complete severance from the rest of India of the north-western and north-eastern zones, in which Moslems constitute a majority, and their establishment as completely independent states controlling their own defence, foreign affairs and finance. I am not concerned here to discuss the immense practical difficulties in the way of the so-called Pakistan project, stated in this its extreme form. Nor need I go back to the dismal record of India's history in the eighteenth century or to the disastrous experience of the Balkan peoples before our eyes, in order to point out the terrible dangers inherent in the break-up of the essential unity of India in its relation to the outside world, a unity of whose achievement we have every right to feel proud. It is enough for my purpose if I can impress upon the House, on the one hand, the underlying determination of Moslem India not to accept any Constitution which does not give reasonably free play to the individual life of the predominantly Moslem units, and, on the other, the growing danger of the preaching on both sides of extreme and incompatible policies.

It was the recognition of this danger, as well as the hope that the gravity of the war situation might bring the parties together in a spirit of responsibility and of co-operation, that led His Majesty's Government to make the new statement of policy which was made public in August last. What was the essence of that statement? It was that the framework of India's future Constitution should be devised, not by this House, but by Indians for themselves. That was a far-reaching and, indeed, revolutionary announcement, the full importance of which has not, I think, even yet been fully appreciated in this country or in India. It was in effect, a recognition in advance of India's status as a Dominion. That recognition was coupled with two conditions. One was that provision would have to be made for the due fulfilment of the obligations which Great Britain's long connexion with India has imposed on her. Some of these such as, for instance, the obligations towards existing members of the services, are by their nature terminable. Others like those arising from India's present dependence upon this country for her defence will naturally be subject to modification with the growth of India's own capacity to defend herself unaided. Others, such as the treaty obligations of the Crown towards the Indian Princes are of a more enduring character. In any case they none of them need stand in the way of shaping the permanent structure of India's future Constitution which is to be essentially an Indian Constitution framed in accordance with Indian conceptions of Indian conditions and of Indian needs.

Even more important in this connexion is the stipulation that the Constitution itself, and the body which is to frame that Constitution, must be the outcome of agreement between the principal elements in India's national life. That is an essential prerequisite to the success of the future Constitution. For if Indians cannot agree upon the kind of Constitution they are prepared to work, how are they likely to agree upon the actual working of it? Our Constitution here works because there is behind it an unwritten agreement based on a tradition of centuries as to the limits within which a majority can exercise its position of advantage. In federal Constitutions everywhere previous free agreement upon the nature of the Constitution and of the limits within which majority rule can be exercised has been the condition upon which the various elements of the federations have come together. Anxious as we are to see the responsibility of Indian government resting on Indian shoulders we can only transfer that responsibility to some authority which can assume it without immediately breaking down or breaking up.

Subject to that requisite of agreement, a requisite inherent in the circumstances of the Indian situation and not arbitrarily imposed by ourselves, the whole field is open for the modification or fundamental reconstruction of the existing Act. Indian statesmen need not be bound either by the system of government at the Centre contemplated in that Act, or by the relations between that Centre and the Provinces and States. If they consider that agreement can be promoted by a redistribution of powers or by a re-arrangement of boundaries, or by changes in the electoral system, that is for them to discuss and settle. If they come to the conclusion that our type of democracy with an Executive dependent upon a parliamentary majority stands in the way of agreement, and that India's needs would be better met by an Executive deriving its authority more directly from the federated units and, like the American Executive, independent of the legislature, that again is their responsibility.

We who in this House wrestled for months with the intricacies of the existing Act—which I still regard as a great piece of constructive legislation, should be the last to underrate the difficulty of the task which lies before Indian statesmanship. It is a task calling for sheer hard thinking in the working out of practical ways and means of solving an immensely complicated problem. It is a task which calls above all for that moderating mediating spirit without which great ends cannot be achieved in human affairs. That is the task we have invited Indian statesmanship to take in hand. While the decisive resolution of so fundamental an issue obviously cannot take place in the midst of the life and death struggle in which we are engaged, there is nothing whatever to prevent Indian political leaders, Indian thinkers, Indian business men, engaging now in those preliminary discussions and studies which are so essential to success and which, no more in India than elsewhere, can be hastily disposed of. We at any rate are only too anxious to promote such study and discussion in every way possible. But the responsibility, both for the initiation and for the completion of this high inquiry, rests with Indians themselves. We can only pledge ourselves to hasten to the utmost degree decisions on all relevant issues that depend upon us. But it is upon Indian statesmen, in the main, and not upon us, that the time-table of future constitutional progress depends.

So much for the major constitutional problem. There was the further question whether, in the interval, there was any practical step that the Government could take which, without prejudging the major issue, could contribute towards its solution. There could, of course, be no question of changing over the whole basis of administrative and legislative power in the supreme crisis of the war, or of placing the direction of India's war effort in the hands of an entirely new executive. Nor, indeed, could that be done without at once raising those very issues of the division of power between the conflicting elements in India which are still unresolved. What we could do was to invite Indian leaders, representing the main political factors, to join the Viceroy's Executive Council. The invitation to them was not only individually to take charge of important departments of State but also to partake fully in the collective responsibility of the Council. Their inclusion would have brought the Indian membership of the Council, official and unofficial, up to a substantial majority of the whole. But it would not have so altered the essential character of the Council as to deprive the Governor-General of his existing trusted advisers, or as to commit the Indian leaders who joined it to any course which would have deprived them of a free hand in dealing with the major problems of the constitutional future. We believed and still believe, that it would give real power and valuable experience to men who have hitherto been in political opposition. Above all we hoped, and still hope, that the creation of such a coalition executive, bringing the older and the newer elements together, would afford an opportunity for Indian leaders, in the atmosphere of the common effort for India's security, to forget their differences and begin to envisage their problems in the light of a wider Indian patriotism.

Our hopes have, so far, been disappointed. Congress rejected out of hand both our major and our interim proposals. Its attitude is 'all or nothing' and by all it means the immediate independence of an India governed by a Constitution which would insure Congress control. It refused even to discuss the matter and proceeded to launch a curious campaign of Mr Gandhi's devising. In pursuance of that campaign Congress leaders, including ex-premiers and ex-ministers, as well as selected members of the rank and file, have made speeches intended and calculated to interfere with the war effort. They have deliberately challenged fine or imprisonment with the same unquestioning obedience to the party whip, as when they resigned office in the Provinces, and in many cases I believe the same misgiving and reluctance. The situation thus created is naturally embarrassing, as it was meant to be. But clearly the Government cannot punish ordinary offenders and overlook the same offences when committed by men whose position and course of action deliberately enhances their significance and their political effect.

This campaign of civil disobedience by instalments has now been in progress for nearly six months. The first phase, in which illegal action was confined to the most prominent members of Congress, ended in January. The second phase, which included representatives of Provincial and local committees, ended early this month, and we are now in the rank and file phase. Magistrates, while vindicating the law, have treated the problem with commonsense, ignoring nonentities, and, in many cases, imposing a fine without the option of imprisonment. This latter procedure has been so discouraging to those whose chief inducement was the prospective electioneering value of a prison sentence that Mr Gandhi has had to announce that the payment of a fine will count as an equally meritorious sacrifice in the Congress cause. On the whole the movement has proceeded languidly and without evoking much popular interest, except in the

United Provinces, which have in recent months contributed more than half the offences. By the middle of March some 7,000 offenders had been convicted, of whom some 5,000 were still in prison. The whole business is as regrettable as it is irrational. But the Government had, and has, no alternative to enforcing the law.

Apart from Congress, the Government's major policy for the constitutional future may be said to have relieved the anxieties of the various elements which compose India's national structure. As regards the more immediate policy of the expansion of the Viceroy's Council, acceptance in principle unfortunately did not lead to actual agreement in detail. The Moslem League, in particular, asked for a measure of representation as against the Hindu elements, and made stipulations as to the future, which the Viceroy could not see his way to accepting. It was, of course, always open to the Viceroy to add to his Council individual Indians of high character and ability. But such a course would not have achieved the desired object, which was to associate representative Hindu and Moslem political leaders with the conduct of the war and so bring them closer together for the future. Very reluctantly, therefore, Lord Linlithgow decided in November to discontinue, for the time being at any rate, his unwearied efforts to bring the various parties together, leaving the door open to further reconsideration by those directly concerned.

No one can regard the present deadlock with satisfaction, least of all patriotic Indians who, looking beyond the narrower aims of sectional leaders, are concerned with India's progress towards that equal partnership in our family of free nations which is alike their goal and ours. They, better than any one else, can help to find a solution. But—and I must add this—they can do so only if they direct their efforts to the real source of the difficulty. In the last few weeks that distinguished veteran statesman, Sir Tej Bahadur Sapru, whose breadth of outlook and courageous initiative played no small part in the deliberations which resulted in the existing federal scheme, brought together in Bombay a number of eminent Indian public men outside the two main contending political organizations to consider the situation. In the end a resolution was passed—though I am not quite clear as to how many of those who attended actually concurred in it—which has since been discussed by Sir Tej with the Viceroy and submitted to His Majesty's Government. The resolution asked for a complete reconstruction of the Executive Council, converting it into one consisting entirely of unofficial Indians drawn from important elements in public life. This new Council should be responsible, while the war is still in progress, to the Crown, and not to the Legislature, but should in substance be treated in regard to all inter-Imperial and international matters on the same footing as a Dominion Government. The reconstruction should be accompanied by the announcement of a specified time limit within which India is to attain to the same measure of freedom as is enjoyed by the Dominions.

I should be the last to approach in a critical or unsympathetic spirit proposals brought forward by men of such eminent public service as have associated themselves with this resolution, or animated with such a genuine desire both to promote India's constitutional progress and her active participation in the common effort. I will, therefore, only touch briefly on some of the more obvious difficulties which such a scheme, if carried into effect, would present in practice. It would amount, not to the modification of the present system of government, but to its supersession by an entirely different type of government. That is certainly something going beyond what we think practicable in the midst of the ever-increasing strain and urgency of the war situation. But it would also create internal constitutional problems of no little difficulty both in relation to the Provinces, whether self-governing or subject to the resolutions which I am moving today, and to the Princes, and in that and other ways raise the still unresolved issues of the constitutional future.

That, indeed, brings me to the underlying issue raised but not faced by the Bombay Resolution. If I may say so without discourtesy to those who have sponsored it, the resolution seems to me to have been directed to the wrong address. I have already pointed out that the time-table of India's constitutional advance depends far more upon Indian agreement than upon ourselves. But the same applies to any far-reaching alteration of the present constitutional position. As I have already made clear, our existing proposal for the expansion of the Viceroy's Council is in suspense, not because those concerned, outside of Congress, condemned the proposal on the score of inadequacy, but mainly because of the difficulty of reconciling Moslem and Hindu claims for relative position. That difficulty is not lessened but inevitably enhanced by any suggestion of a new type of Executive with more extensive powers. It is unfortunately evident that Sir Tej Sapru and his friends have not been able to secure beforehand for their scheme any kind of agreement, if not between Congress and the Moslem League, at any rate between the latter and other representatives of the Hindu majority. Mr Jinnah, the leader of the Moslem League, has since repudiated the scheme as being on 'entirely wrong lines' and as a trap into which Sir Tej had been led by 'Congress wire-pullers'. The General Secretary of the Mahasabha Party, on the other hand, has declared that it will not co-operate in any scheme in which the numerical majority of the Hindu element is not reflected in the composition of the Council. There is obviously no such agreement here as would afford the reconstructed Council political support or even acquiescence in the Legislature.

On the other hand, if the reconstructed Council is to be composed, not of leaders who between them can secure some measure of political backing, but of men individually eminent but unsupported, then the objections which weighed against that course in the case of an expansion of the existing Council, become much more formidable if it is a question of an entirely new Council with greatly enlarged powers. It would, I think, be very difficult to persuade Parliament to confer Dominion or quasi-Dominion powers on a body so constituted. Nor would such a body, between their responsibility to the Crown on one side and in face of an unfriendly legislature on the other, be likely for long to maintain its precarious position.

My appeal to Sir Tej and his friends would therefore be not to cease from their efforts, but to concentrate, first and foremost, upon bringing the contending elements in India together. Whether they can best do that by the exercise of their persuasion upon the existing party leaders, or by building up a strong central party of men who are prepared to put India first, their effort may well be decisive in shaping the whole future of their country.

Meanwhile there are other fields besides that of politics in which India's future is being shaped. In Africa, in Malaya and now in Iraq, India is establishing her claim to consideration as a major factor in the winning of the war. Her troops have by their gallantry and technical efficiency made a conspicuous contribution to our victories in Libya and Eritrea. They have faced the trying ordeal of modern war, largely under the leadership of Indian officers who have amply justified their training and the confidence placed in them. Her young Navy has earned the highest commendation from the Admiralty—no easy critics—for its indefatigable work in the seas east of Suez. The expansion of her infant Air Force is only held back by the imperative needs elsewhere of a still inadequate total supply of machines. Her industries have already made an unprecedented contribution to her war effort and ours in every kind of military supply. Thanks to the stimulating energies of Sir Alexander Roger's technical mission and to the policy of mutual co-operation with her neighbours set on foot by the Delhi Conference and continued by the Eastern Group Supply Council, they will do so on an ever-increasing scale as the war progresses. All these things constitute a real and indefeasible advance in that progress towards self-dependence and true equality which constitutional developments can and should confirm, but which they cannot of themselves create if the basic conditions are not there.

Our desire in this House, shared by all parties, is that India should advance, and advance rapidly, all along the line in the indispensable prerequisites to the fullest conceivable measure of freedom. From that point of view we welcome, with pride, her achievements in war as evidence of her growing capacity to meet her own defence. We welcome the industrial progress which will not only subserve the needs of that defence, but contribute to her general economic strength. We should welcome even more, perhaps, any measures that can raise the standard of nutrition and health of the vast agricultural majority of a population which has, with an almost staggering increase, risen from 350 to 400 millions in the last decade. We welcome, above all, every effort that Indians can make to come together and find a solution to India's complex and difficult problem which will do justice alike to the claims of her diverse elements for a due recognition of their individuality, and to the need of that wider unity which is essential to her peace and prosperity.

I have dwelt today, deliberately, upon Indian responsibility in this matter, for unless Indians are prepared to face that responsibility now they will fail to face it hereafter. Agreement imposed by us from without cannot survive the withdrawal of our power to enforce it. Only a real agreement, freely reached, can stand that test. It is for Indian statesmen to find that measure of agreement which is indispensable if we, on our side, are to make our further contribution towards the completion of our own task in India, the task of joining with them in crowning peace and unity with freedom.

X

EXPANSION OF THE EXECUTIVE COUNCIL

HOUSE OF COMMONS, AUGUST 1st, 1941

On Tuesday of last week I made a brief statement on the recent expansion of the Viceroy's Executive Council and on the formation of an All-India National Defence Council. The purpose of today's Debate, as I understand it, is to enable me to explain, in somewhat fuller detail, the nature and purpose of these measures, and to afford opportunities for their discussion in relation to the general Indian policy of His Majesty's Government. In order to understand that policy, it is essential that the Committee should keep clearly in mind the fundamental change which has come over the whole Indian problem since those long discussions which preceded the passing of the present Government of India Act six years ago. The whole issue in debate in those days was whether, and, if so, how far, this country could, or should, transfer its authority for the government of India as a whole to Indian hands. That was the issue as between Indian political leaders and this House. That was also the issue on which we ourselves were most keenly divided. That issue, as an issue of principle, has passed outside the field of controversy. It is today a matter of general acceptance that India should, as soon as is practicable, attain to Dominion status, or, as I prefer to describe it, to free and equal partnership in our British Commonwealth. How far that policy is to be expedited, what provision will still have to be made for the carrying out of obligations imposed upon us by the past or by India's present dependence on this country for her defence —those are matters which, however important in themselves, are still matters of detail and method rather than of fundamental principle.

Today the major issue is not whether India should

govern herself, but how is she to govern herself; under what type of Constitution is it possible to preserve her unity and yet secure freedom and reasonable self-expression for the varied elements which compose her national life? Six years ago that issue had hardly loomed over the horizon. We knew, of course, that there was a communal problem, and we assumed that we had met it by providing a separate communal franchise. We knew there were the hesitations of the Princes as to their powers, and we provided specially favourable terms to induce them to come in. But we and Indian political leaders alike took it for granted that the Central Government of India should follow the customary lines of our British system of responsible Parliamentary Government, and the Act of 1935 was framed on that assumption.

The course of events since then, experience in the actual working of responsible government in the Provinces, has raised the most formidable queries as to the possibility of that system in India, at any rate so far as the Central Government of India is concerned. We must remember that our system of government here, which we rightly prize as the most flexible and efficient form of democracy in the world, that system which seems to us so natural and so easily workable, does depend entirely for its working upon certain indispensable conditions. It postulates a party system in which loyalty to party is never the supreme loyalty, but is always in the last resort subordinate to a sense of loyalty to the national interests as a whole and to responsibility for the working of Parliament. That system of ours is based on majority decision, because it assumes that the majority is in every case the result of free discussion, and that the minorities today will very probably be the majorities to-morrow. Where these conditions do not exist, where party loyalty and party discipline override all other considerations, where party executives outside Parliament are the only arbiters of policy and the real rulers, where the minority always remain the underdog—there our system ceases to be workable and other methods have to be devised to preserve freedom and democracy.

In India, experience of party government has, rightly

or wrongly, convinced great and powerful elements in Indian national life that their rights and their liberties would not be assured under the central provisions of the present Act, or, indeed, under any amendment of it, but would still leave the executive control of all India in the hands of a Government dependent upon a Parliamentary majority from day to day, a majority which in turn obeys unswervingly the dictates of an outside body. This reaction against the danger of what is called a Congress Raj or Hindu Raj has gone so far as to lead to a growing demand from Moslem quarters for the complete breaking-up of India into separate Hindu and Moslem dominions. I need say nothing today of the manifold and, to my mind, insuperable objections to such a scheme, at any rate in its extreme form. I would only note this, that it merely shifts the problem of permanent minorities to somewhat smaller areas without solving it. It is a counsel of despair and, I believe, of wholly unnecessary despair, for I do not doubt that there is enough constructive ability and enough good will among Hindus and Moslems, and enough Indian patriotism, to find a constitutional solution which will give fair recognition to all interests.

That, at any rate, was the conclusion embodied in the declaration—a far-reaching declaration—which His Majesty's Government made in August last, and which was announced to India by Lord Linlithgow. Responding to the widespread criticism of the Act of 1935, which was imposed upon India by Parliament here, it invited Indians, by agreement among themselves, to devise the framework of the Indian Constitution in accordance with the social, economic, and political structure of Indian life. While the resulting new Constitution could not, in our view, be set in operation in the midst of our present struggle for existence, the declaration promised every help to enable matters to be brought to a conclusion with the least possible delay after the war, as well as to promote every sincere and practical step that representative Indians might take, meanwhile, to arrive at agreement.

Let me make that point clear. The problem is not an easy one, and even if there were no war, finding an agreed solution would be bound to take time in India, as it has everywhere else. All the more reason then, it seems to me, for Indians to get together now to make a beginning on this high inquiry. It is an essential matter for them, because it affects their relations among themselves and also because the right and the responsibility for doing so come naturally with the claim to self-government. That declaration came as a welcome assurance to Moslems and other important elements that their fate would not be settled over their heads by some bargaining between the Government here and the Congress Party. On the other hand, it is perfectly true that it did come as a shock not only to Congress but also to many other moderate elements in India and even here, because it made clear that a new stage must inevitably intervene before India could obtain her goal. It is not infrequently the climber's fate in the high mountains when, after hours of arduous toil up steep and difficult rock he reaches what he believed to be the summit, only to find that the real summit lies further back, separated, very possibly, by a narrow and treacherous ridge of snow or ice. He finds that a new effort, less strenuous perhaps but calling for even greater skill and a new technique is still required of him before the final victory. Just so it seems to me there is today a call on Indian statesmen for a new and different effort, for a new technique of consultation and conciliation with each other rather than that of addressing demands to this House or belabouring the Government of India.

In these new conditions of technique civil disobedience cuts no ice because it bears no relation to the real issues. On the other hand, I need not say that I welcome most sincerely the resolution which was passed at Poona by a conference of non-party leaders urging their chairman, Sir Tej Bahadur Sapru, to take steps immediately to initiate an examination of the problem of the future Constitution of a united India. No Indian statesman is better qualified than Sir Tej Bahadur Sapru to address himself both to the actual constitutional problem itself and to the many personal elements which have to be brought together and reconciled before a solution can be found. In this connexion I should like to correct a misapprehension which, judging by the terms of another resolution passed by the same conference, seems to have been entertained in some quarters. It is that in insisting upon agreement between the principal elements in India's national life, we were thinking only of the major political parties. The main elements in Indian national life include not only political organizations and the great religious and cultural communities of India; they also include geographical and administrative entities, the Provinces of British India, more especially those which have not thrown away the responsibility for self-government, and the Indian States. Nor is the substantial agreement which we wish to see achieved necessarily dependent on the fiat of party leaders.

That brings me to the other half of the policy announced last August. Having deliberately, and I venture to say rightly and even necessarily, remitted to Indian hands the framing of India's future Constitution, His Majesty's Government wished as an interim policy, and within the framework of the existing Constitution, to associate Indian leaders more closely, more intimately and more responsibly with the government of their country during the war. We wished to do so in order to emphasize the undoubted unity of purpose between India and ourselves in the present struggle against the evil forces which are just as hateful to every section in India as they are to ourselves, and also for the defence of India's own existence. At the same time we also cherished the hope that in the process of working together for the common cause Indian statesmen would find new bonds of mutual understanding and of union which would help towards a solution of their constitutional problem. Our interim policy was, indeed, conceived as the most practical contribution we could make at this stage towards the goal in view. It prejudged no constitutional issue. It committed no one who co-operated in it to anything beyond his individual co-operation in the war effort. But it would afford a wider range of administrative responsibility and experience to Indian public men and be, at any rate, an earnest of our desire to see the Government of India increasingly entrusted to Indian hands.

It was with these objects in view that Lord Linlithgow was authorized to enlarge his Executive Council, so as to make it comprise a majority of Indian members, and at the same time to set up a War Advisory Council which would serve as a means of contact between the Central Government and the local war effort all over India, including the Indian States. For his enlarged Executive Council the Viceroy naturally turned, in the first instance, to the leaders of the political parties. He could hope, by enlisting their co-operation, to secure automatically a wide measure of support from the Legislature, as well as from the political organizations throughout the country. In that hope Lord Linlithgow was disappointed. Congress rejected co-operation out of hand, refusing even to discuss the matter, and launched their futile campaign of challenging imprisonment by the delivery of speeches calculated and intended to impede the war effort. The other main parties, Moslem and Hindu, while accepting in principle, put forward conflicting claims and stipulations which it was impossible for the Viceroy to reconcile. In the end, Lord Linlithgow was compelled reluctantly to admit that even his unwearied efforts—and I may remind hon. Members that they have been carried on ever since the beginning of the war—to bring the party leaders together could not succeed in face of their mutual jealousies and suspicions.

That did not mean an abandonment of his policy. As I stated last August, the Viceroy was determined, if the leaders remained un-co-operative, to go ahead, prepared to work with those who were ready to work with him and with each other. On every hand, too, evidence reached Lord Linlithgow of growing public annoyance in India with purely partisan manœuvres and of a growing sense of frustration that these manœuvres should be allowed to prevent the great body of competent and able Indians, willing to co-operate in the war effort, and thus express the desire of the vast majority of Indian people, from serving their country in its hour of need. The conference that met in Bombay last March, under the chairmanship of Sir Tej Sapru, clearly voiced that sense of frustration. So did our last Debate in the House. Their demands, though expressed in a form, as I ventured to point out in the Debate on April 22nd, open to serious practical objection, still expressed a spirit with which both the Viceroy and myself were largely in sympathy, and to which we were resolved to give effect.

Accordingly, Lord Linlithgow, leaving the parties to pursue their own controversies, decided to address himself directly to those Indian public men who, as individuals, were by their ability or their essentially representative character best fitted to strengthen the Government both in the actual work of administration and in the eyes of the public, and to appeal to them to come forward and, putting India first, play their part in the conduct of India's defence. How rightly he judged the public temper and the character of Indian public men will be apparent from the fact that, with hardly an exception, all those whom he approached in the first instance as the men best qualified for the task that he had in view, responded unhesitatingly and without regard to previous party affiliations.

India is at war, and the menace of war may well draw closer to her frontiers, both from the East and from the West within the next few months. Consequently, the governing consideration in the expansion of the Viceroy's Executive—his War Cabinet, if I may use the term—was necessarily efficiency. From that point of view there was, in any case, the strongest justification for the separation, under war conditions, of portfolios which had been previously combined, as well as for the creation of special new departments, such as Civil Defence and Information.

I notice that the Viceroy has been criticized in some quarters on the ground that he has not appointed the new Indian members to the so-called key posts of finance and defence. I do not think that criticism will find much echo in the House, where we fully realize the extent to which, in war time, at any rate, Supply and Labour, Civil Defence and Information are vital departments. For these undoubtedly key positions, Lord Linlithgow has selected the men whom he believed individually best fitted for the work in hand—a great industrialist like Sir Hormusji Mody for Supply; experienced ex-Ministers and administrators like Mr Rao and Sir Firozkhan Noon for the Departments of Civil Defence and Labour; an elder statesman of unrivalled experience and authority like Sir Akbar Hydari for Information; an independent and courageous party politician (of the Left, I may say) like Mr Aney for a lighter department but for the work of the Legislature. Two further appointments were made necessary by the promotion to the Federal Court of Sir Muhammad Zafrullah Khan, succeeded by another eminent lawyer, Sir Sultan Ahmed, and by the transfer of Sir Girja Bajpai to the very interesting newly created post of Indian Agent-General in Washington, attached to the British Embassy, with the rank and status of Minister Plenipotentiary—a fresh indication of India's growing importance and status—succeeded by Mr Nalini Sarkar, recently Finance Minister in Bengal. To attempt to make so small a body as the Executive representative of all the different elements of India's national life would obviously have been impossible. The important thing was to find a team of individual competence and ability and willing to share the collective work and responsibility of the Executive, and in this, I venture to say, Lord Linlithgow has definitely succeeded.

The old Executive contained, apart from the Viceroy, four European and three Indian members. In the new Executive there will be eight Indians to four European members, a majority of two to one, a development which marks a change not perhaps in the form, but at any rate in the spirit of our Indian administration. The National Defence Council, on the other hand, will, except for the presence of one representative of the European commercial community and another of the resident Anglo-Indian community, be entirely Indian in composition. This National Defence Council is essentially a body representative of all the elements, communal, local, political, of the whole national life of India; of India in the fullest sense of the word, for on it will be nine representatives of the Indian States whose rulers have shown their patriotism and their loyalty in such full measure during the present war. The twenty-two members from British India include representatives not only of the different Provinces and communities, but also of industry, commerce and agriculture. Labour is effectively represented both by Dr Ambedkar, the unwearied champion of the Scheduled Castes, which include so large a proportion of the most depressed elements of the working classes, and by Mr Jamnadas Mehta, who represents the railway workers. Nor must I pass, without mentioning the inclusion of a representative of the women's interests in the shape of the Begum Shah Nawaz. It would, I think, have been difficult by any process to secure a better cross-section or microcosm of India's national life in all its rich variety.

It may be said that this is not a truly representative body because its members owe their position to the personal invitation of the Viceroy and not directly to popular election, and also because the largest and most highly organized political party has deliberately excluded itself. It is, I think, worth while pointing out, in answer to that criticism, that of the twenty-two British Indian members no fewer than sixteen are elected members of their legislatures, including four Prime Ministers, and if those great Provinces, Bengal, the Punjab, Assam and Sind, with a population of more than 100,000,000 souls, are not represented by their Prime Ministers, I do not know who could claim to represent them. It is perfectly true that Congress, in its present mood, is not represented, but a very considerable proportion of the members—and this applies to the Executive Council as well as to the National Defence Council—have been closely associated with Congress in the past, and, if they have recently differed from the political tactics of the Congress High Command, that does not mean that they are in any sense less genuine in the strength of their national convictions. The National Defence Council is in no sense a collection of 'Yes-men', scraped together by the Viceroy in order to produce a facade of Indian support. It is a body of patriotic Indians who have readily come forward to help their country at a critical juncture. This National Defence Council is an advisory body, and its main purpose is to bring the war effort in the Provinces and States, as well as in the ranks of commerce, industry, and labour, into more direct and effective touch with the Central Government. It will meet periodically under the Viceroy's chairmanship, both to be informed of, and to discuss, the course of events and the policy of the Government, and to convey to the Government the suggestions and needs of the localities or interests they represent.

There will thus be a continual contact and exchange of views and information both ways, between the Viceroy and his Executive, and the Provincial or State Governments, local war committees or industrial organizations, which should be most helpful in guiding and in stimulating India's war effort. I might add further, as an instance of the anxiety of the Indian Government to procure the closest possible contact with public opinion and to strengthen the Indian element in the administration, the creation on the initiative of the late Commander-in-Chief, General Sir Claude Auchinleck, since confirmed by General Wavell, of a Defence Committee of the Legislature in order to keep members in touch with the work of the Defence Departments, and the appointment of a very able Indian official as joint secretary of that Department. These measures have not brought about any change in the existing Constitution of India. Even if it were possible to change the basis of power and authority in the middle of a crisis so menacing to India's very existence, no such transfer would be feasible without some measure of agreement, such as, unfortunately, does not exist today, as to the kind of Constitution under which the various main elements of India's national life would be willing to work together.

The immediate object of these measures has been to increase the efficiency of government, and at the same time to make fuller use of a vast and so far untapped reservoir of Indian ability and patriotism. At the same time they are an earnest of our desire to transfer to Indian hands a steadily increasing share in the control of India's destiny. They mark a change in the spirit, if not in the letter, of India's Constitution. Above all, I hope, in all sincerity, that the coming together of all these distinguished representatives of every element in India's diversified and politically conflicting life may have made, at least, a beginning in breaking the political deadlock between Indians which has assumed so disquieting and, on the face of it, increasingly intractable a character. If Indians can drop considerations of party and communal rivalry in order to protect India from external danger in war, surely it should not be impossible for them to come together to find ways and means of saving her from the even greater danger which threatens her from internal strife, and of removing, in the process, the main obstacles to the attainment of her rightful position as a free and equal partner in the British Commonwealth.

It is in that hope—not overstated, I trust, for I fully recognize all the efforts of good will and of sheer constructive thought that must yet be made—that I commend to the House the measures which we have taken. I should not wish to quarrel for a moment with those who, either in this House or in India, think these measures inadequate because they do not involve those direct constitutional changes which seem to me, for the reasons I have given, impossible to bring about at this stage without intensifying India's internal difficulties. All I would ask is that the young plant which the Viceroy has with such unwearied care seeded and set in the ground, should be given the opportunity to grow, and the opportunity to fulfil the immediate task for which it was intended, and, it may be, also to develop latent possibilities of further benefit to India in directions we cannot yet foresee. Meanwhile I hope, whatever criticisms of the general policy of His Majesty's Government may be expressed—and they naturally and properly will be expressed in this House today—that nothing will be said which can be calculated to discourage the men who have come forward to serve India, or to weaken their hands in the high task to which they have set themselves for India's sake.

XI

THE STAFFORD CRIPPS MISSION

HOUSE OF COMMONS, APRIL 28TH, 1942

ALL the speakers have paid a just tribute to my right hon. and learned Friend the Lord Privy Seal (Sir Stafford Cripps) for the conspicuous ability, sincerity, and, not least, good temper with which he discharged his difficult Mission. No more fitting ambassador could have been sent, not only because of his position as a member of the War Cabinet, but also because his sending marked in a peculiar degree the unity of outlook and policy with regard to India which has been reached by the Government, and, I might add, by Parliament and public opinion in this country. I say advisedly 'reached' because the Mission and the unanimous policy for which my right hon. and learned Friend endeavoured to secure acceptance were not a sudden improvisation to meet a critical external situation—the death-bed repentance of an unregenerate Imperialism. They were the natural and, indeed, inevitable culmination of a steady development, during these last few years, of thought and feeling about India and Indian political aspirations.

The Act of 1935, which was so fiercely contested at the time, was a great piece of constructive statesmanship which might by now have carried India far on the road towards complete freedom if it could have been promptly implemented. But we have all along since moved beyond it. We no longer think in terms of India's progressive advance towards full control of her own destiny by stages decided here and under a Constitution laid down by this House. We think, instead, in terms of India's inherent right to that freedom under a Constitution of her own devising. It is because Indian leaders have, I think, not fully realized hitherto, or not fully believed in, this change of our outlook in its bearing upon their relations both to ourselves and to each other, that the Mission of my right hon. and learned Friend has, I believe, been of such permanent value for the future, whatever its immediate outcome.

The primary task assigned to my right hon. and learned Friend was to remove all doubts as to the sincerity of our purpose. We had already declared, at the very outset almost of the career of the present Government, that we wished India to attain the same full freedom as is enjoyed by the Dominions and, for that matter, by ourselves, and to do so as soon as possible after the war under a Constitution of Indian devising.[1] That pledge was subject only to two stipulations. One stipulation was that the Constitution should provide for the due fulfilment of the obligations imposed on us by our historic connexion with India. The other was that the Constitution should carry with it the acceptance of the principal elements in India's national life. Indian political opinion was not prepared to believe that we really meant what we said. It read into the stipulation about obligations an intention to superimpose on the Constitution conditions and safeguards which would, in effect, make it no longer the Constitution of a free country—to take back with one hand what we professed to give with the other. Again, it read into the stipulation about agreement a cynical acquiescence in the indefinite continuance of disagreement and, consequently, of the present regime in India.

The main object of the draft Declaration[2] was to set these suspicions at rest. The full meaning of Dominion independence was set out in the preamble in terms taken from the famous Balfour Declaration of 1926. Moreover, as my right hon. and learned Friend has already pointed out, the provision in Section (*c*) for settling by treaty all matters arising out of the complete transfer of responsibility from British to Indian hands not only emphasized Indian equality of status, but expressly laid down that the terms of the treaty should not restrict the power of the future Indian Union to decide its relationship to the rest of the Empire, in other words, restrict

[1] See Appendix I. [2] See Appendix II.

its *de facto* power to secede from the Commonwealth. How could we have gone further than that ?

Again, in order to meet the charge that we deliberately wished to postpone a settlement we put forward two suggestions. One was that, failing previous agreement between the leaders of Indian opinion in the principal communities on some other form of Constitution-making body, we would set up the one defined in Section (*d*) of the draft Declaration immediately on the cessation of hostilities. The other point was to answer the charge that we were giving the minorities, and more particularly the Moslem element, a veto on all progress. There was only one way of cutting that Gordian knot, and that was to tell the majority that they were free to go ahead and achieve full freedom without waiting for the minority. It was made equally clear to the Moslem minority—an element, I might add, of over 90,000,000 people—that, if, in the last resort, they could not find the Constitution of the new Indian Union acceptable to themselves, either at the outset or upon further reconsideration, they were not to be denied the prospect of an equal freedom.

In this respect we were only following a familiar Dominion precedent. The Canadian Federation was originally formed by four only of the present Provinces. Others joined in the next few years. On the other hand, Newfoundland has always remained outside. The Australian Commonwealth and the South African Union afford similar examples of making special conditions for entering or else standing out altogether. In the case of India, the Act of 1935 left the States free to stay out, but provided for the adhesion of a minimum number of States before the federal provisions of the Act came into force. This restrictive provision also was practically waived in the draft Declaration. Our ideal undoubtedly remains a united all-India including the States as well as British India, sufficiently united at any rate to present a common front to the outside world. The unity which we have given to India, a unity of law, of administrative procedure, of economic and transport policy, is an achievement of which we have every right to be proud, but we would sooner see India divided and free than keep her various elements for ever chafing against us and against each other under a sense of impotent frustration.

The practical arguments for unity are undoubtedly overwhelming. I have little doubt that they would prevail if it were not for the deep-seated fear of the Moslems, to which my right hon. Friend the Member for Horsham (Earl Winterton) eloquently referred, that their distinctive culture and way of life would be at the mercy of a permanent Hindu majority. The root of that fear, which, as my hon. Friend the Member for Aylesbury (Sir S. Reed) said, we must banish, lies largely, I believe, in the assumption so often made that unity implies a Central Executive on the British model, an Executive responsible in theory to a Parliamentary majority, but responsible, in fact, to the party caucus behind that majority. Yet our British system, which we have developed in a homogeneous country, is not necessarily the best suited to so complex a structure as that of India. There is no sealed pattern of freedom. The United States, Switzerland, the former Germanic and Austro-Hungarian Federations, and the Union of Soviet Socialist Republics may all supply useful precedents for Indian statesmanship to study. What, indeed, is needed, perhaps even more than new constitutional methods, is a new spirit of compromise. It is by making Indian statesmen conscious that the solution of the problem is their own undivided responsibility and not ours that both the right methods and the right spirit are most likely to emerge.

Our main concern was to indicate a solution for the future which left no doubt as to our own intentions and which struck as fair a balance between contending points of view as it was possible to attain. We did so because it was only in the light of a solution recognized as essentially sincere and fair, even if not wholly acceptable to any one section, that there could be any hope of the co-operation in the present of Indian political leaders either with ourselves or with each other to face the crisis in front of India. Even so, it could only be a question of co-operation, of 'effective participation and of active and constructive help'—to quote the language of the draft Declaration—within the existing Constitution. It could not be a question of control, free from the ultimate responsibility of Parliament here, exercised through the Secretary of State and the Viceroy. It could not be that, both for the practical reasons which have been given in connexion with defence by my right hon. and learned Friend, but above all for the reason that there was no agreement as to who should exercise that control.

The demand for a National Government put forward by Congress has been repeated in more than one speech in this House. But such a National Government would have been responsible in the last resort neither to Parliament here, under the existing Constitution, nor to an agreed and fairly balanced Constitution in India, but only to its own majority—a majority, presumably, of Congress or at any rate of Hindus. That demand, whether made by Sir Tej Bahadur Sapru and his colleagues or by Congress, was the one thing which the Moslems and other minorities were determined at all costs to reject. They were and they are convinced that such a Government would in fact prejudge the whole future situation to their detriment. There was therefore never any question in our view of conceding that demand, because it was in fact, if not in intention, a demand which precluded all agreed co-operation in India.

Within the limits of the ultimate responsibility of the Viceroy and Parliament, who in this matter are trustees for the future Constitution of India, my right hon. and learned Friend was given the widest latitude. Indeed, as the House will have appreciated from the White Paper and from his own speech, he went to the utmost lengths in order to meet the wishes of Congress. There was no more that he could offer. My right hon. and learned Friend has given the House a full and most lucid account of his negotiations and of the reason for their breakdown. I will not cover that ground again. There is only one point that I would add, but it is perhaps the most significant and illuminating point in the whole story. My right hon. and learned Friend flew many thousands of miles to meet the Indian leaders in order to arrive at an agreement with them. The Indian leaders in Delhi moved not one step to meet each other, either without him or in his presence. They made no attempt to reach agreement among themselves. The Congress demand for a National Government was declared by its President to be the 'unanimous demand of the Indian people'. Why then was no attempt made to afford evidence of that unanimity by bringing forward, in concert with the Moslem League and other parties, an agreed proposal? For the simple reason that it could not have been done. That is an aspect of the situation which we must face. We do not do so for the purpose of imputing blame to any Indian section. My hon. Friend the Member for Walsall very truly said that it is by no means an easy matter for men whose whole life has been concentrated in opposition to each other to come to a speedy agreement. Even in this House we had to be at war for many months before a National Government was secured. We have to face this aspect, however, in order to realize why it was impossible for my right hon. and learned Friend to meet the demand for a so-called National Government.

While the Mission of my right hon. and learned Friend failed of its immediate object, in a wider sense I believe it has been very far from a failure. It has been, if I may adopt an epigram of his own, the epilogue of an old chapter, the chapter in which the contending elements in India have attempted to attain their ends by belabouring His Majesty's Government, and also the prologue of a new chapter in which Indians are beginning to realize that the key to India's problems is in their own hands. Since my right hon. and learned Friend left India, Mr Gandhi has summed up that point in a striking statement in which he has declared the attainment of independence impossible until Indians have themselves solved the communal tangle. That declaration is, I think, sufficient answer to speeches which have been made suggesting that it is we who have exaggerated, if not indeed invented, the communal issue.

Mr S. O. Davies: Are the Government accepting all that Gandhi says?

Mr Amery: I accept it when he now says what I have spent two years in saying. Even more important as evidence of a new approach are the resolutions which were passed at the statesmanlike instigation of Mr Rajagopalachari, ex-Premier of Madras, by the Congress members of the Madras Legislature. By the first of these resolutions the All-India Congress Committee was urged to waive its objection to the Moslem League claim for separation, if eventually persisted in, for the sake of removing every obstacle from the way of establishing a national administration. By the second the national All-India Congress Committee was requested to permit an approach to the Moslem League with a view to the re-establishment of popular government in Madras Province. It would appear that this patriotic and courageous declaration has met with the disapproval of the Congress President and Mr Nehru. It may be that their attitude will be sustained by the All-India Committee which is to meet in the next few days. Be that as it may, this new and hopeful initiative has been taken. It would never have been taken but for the visit of my right hon. and learned Friend.

Mr S. O. Davies: How many were present when the resolution was passed? Only 32 out of 200 passed that resolution.

Mr Amery: No; I believe 39 out of 42 present supported it. At any rate, will anybody suggest that it was an undesirable resolution or that the desire on the part of Congress members to come to reasonable terms with their Moslem colleagues to re-establish free government in their Province first, and to make progress with free government for India, was wrong? If only three had supported it, I should honour them for doing so.

It has been asked, what is precisely meant by the withdrawal of the draft Declaration? What we have certainly not withdrawn is our main object and purpose, namely, that India should, as soon as possible, obtain full freedom, under constitutional arrangements of her own devising and suited to her own peculiar conditions. On the other hand, the particular method which we suggested for arriving at a constitutional settlement, more particularly the present Provincial basis, both for setting up a Constitution-making body and for non-accession has not met with sufficient support for us to press it further. It may be that alternative methods can be devised which might afford a better basis for the definition of boundaries for the major elements, and might give representation for the smaller elements, such as the Sikhs, whose natural anxieties we fully appreciate. It is for Indians themselves to improve on our suggestion, if they can.

As regards the interim situation, the particular proposals made by my right hon. and learned Friend in order to secure the whole-hearted co-operation of Congress, as well as of the other political parties, have, of course, lapsed. But the Viceroy will, no doubt, always be willing to consider practical suggestions within the framework of Section (*e*) of the draft Declaration, put forward by responsible party leaders, more particularly if put forward, as the hon. Member for Ince (Mr G. Macdonald) suggested, jointly, and based on a broad measure of agreement. It is, indeed, upon the agreement and initiative of Indian party leaders that any further ,advance must depend. My hon. Friend the Member for Walsall raised the question of the desirability of re-establishing self-government in those Provinces in which Congress has refused to carry it on. That, of course, is most desirable. It would have been a natural consequence of the success of my right hon. and learned Friend's Mission. The door is open now, and it remains open.

MR G. MACDONALD: What exactly does the right hon. Gentleman mean by 'the door remains open'? Supposing the Congress Party in those very Provinces agreed themselves to carry on self-government, would the

British Government agree?

MR AMERY: Yes; if in any of those Provinces the Congress Party are prepared to assume the responsibilities of government and to give that help to the prosecution of the war which they have declared they wish to give, we are only too ready to let them resume office under those conditions.

Meanwhile, the Government of India must get on with the immediate task before them. I must make it quite clear that our anxiety to secure a wider measure of active co-operation from the political parties in India by sending out my right hon. and learned Friend in no way implies any lack of confidence in the ability or energy of the Executive Government of India. On the contrary, His Majesty's Government have the most complete confidence in the Viceroy, Lord Linlithgow, who has handled a continuously difficult situation with prudent wisdom, and whose vigorous initiative has been invaluable in everything bearing on the conduct of the war. That confidence extends no less to the existing Executive Council. The Indian members, who form the majority of that Council, are men of high ability and of experience in active politics, in administration, and in business. Their patriotic willingness to stand aside for others who might command a greater measure of organized political support is something that we have sincerely appreciated, as they, I feel sure, recognize the value which we attach to their continued service to India at this critical time. What I have said of the Indian members applies equally to the European members, and indeed, to the whole of the administrative services, Indian and British, which have wrestled so ably with the innumerable problems created by war conditions.

The hon. Member for Ince and the hon. and gallant Member for South-East Leeds have made the suggestion that the work of the India Office might be transferred to the Dominions Office. I think that that suggestion is based upon a very insufficient realization of the work of the India Office. The main work of the India Office does not consist in controlling, restricting, interfering with India. Its main work is that of an agency in this country on behalf of the Government of India. The Government of India have in peace, and even more in war, a great Army to maintain, part of it directly drawn from this country and the rest largely officered by this country and largely equipped from this country. In order to secure from the Government of this country what India needs, it requires a considerable military staff at this end. India has neighbours which make the foreign policy of this country a matter of vital interest to her. From that point of view again she has to have a considerable staff to keep in touch with the Foreign Office and see that India's interests are not neglected. Further, there is a vast range of economic problems which vitally concern India and with regard to which it is important to her to see that the policy of this country does not neglect Indian interests. All these matters, if India were a self-governing Dominion, would still have to be carried on, but carried on by an enlarged High Commissioner's office like the offices at Australia House and at Canada House. But as long as the ultimate responsibility for these matters rests with the Secretary of State they must be conducted under his immediate eye. He is still what the High Commissioners for the Dominions are, in that sphere at any rate—the chief agent and representative of the Government of India and of the interests of India.

MR G. MACDONALD: This is a very important point. Is this being put forward as a conclusive argument? Are we to understand that a High Commissioner should not do what is now being done by the Secretary of State? Would it not be right to remove the root cause of all the trouble, mistrust, and suspicion and so give an indication of our sincerity?

MR AMERY: The Dominions Office, which deals with diplomatic and not with administrative problems, could handle the former problems for India if the other matters were handed over to a representative of an Indian Dominion Government. But to make in the meanwhile an unreal pretence, administratively impossible, that we were really changing the situation would be a mere sham and camouflage which would fail to impress anyone.

MAJOR MILNER: Has not India a High Commissioner here?

MR AMERY: Yes, for those purposes which are entirely within the discretion of the Government and Legislature of India, and they cover a wide field. But they do not cover the field of those matters which must for the time being still be the responsibility of the Secretary of State.

To come back to India, we rely also no less upon the Commander-in-Chief, Sir Archibald Wavell, and upon all ranks in the Fighting Services of India. The Indian Army has a great tradition, of which those serving in it are justly proud. In this war it has won new glory upon many a hard-fought field. Side by side with it, its record has been shared by troops which the Indian Princes have, with their accustomed loyalty, placed unreservedly at the disposal of the King-Emperor. India's younger Services, the Royal Indian Navy and the Indian Air Force, have already proved their quality and earned high commendation from all whom they have served. It is upon these trained and properly equipped Services, together with their old British and newer Allied comrades in arms, that India must rely for her defence, whether on her outer marches or in the case of actual invasion. In the latter event the Army can undoubtedly receive great help from the general body of the population. The steadfastness of the public in face of danger, its eagerness to co-operate with the military authorities in every way, including the whole field of Civil Defence, the securing of information and in guerrilla operations—all these things can be of invaluable aid to the operations of Regular troops.

We are glad to believe that Indian political leaders are anxious to give that aid, even if they are not prepared to co-operate on the lines which, in our opinion, would give the best results.[1] All the same, it is to the

[1] The All-India Congress Committee, a few days later, decided in favour of 'non-violent' resistance to invasion.

trained officers and men of her Regular Forces, and to their effective and adequate equipment, that India must look for her security now and in the years to come. These were matters into which my right hon. and learned Friend the Lord Privy Seal also looked during his visit to India, and the information and suggestions which he has brought back will be of the greatest value to us. My right hon. and learned Friend's Mission, whatever else it has done—I believe it has done much, as time will show—has at any rate had one immediate effect. It has brought home to the public here and elsewhere something of the complex character of India's political structure and of the inherent obstacles to any simple, off-hand solution. They are not obstacles which should discourage us in our purpose. We have behind us a record of achievement in the building-up of the present structure of the Indian Empire of which we can well afford to be proud. If we can achieve a transfer to Indian shoulders of the responsibilities for the maintenance of that fabric, if we can play our part in the transformation of an administrative machine into a free and self-reliant national life, we shall have even better reason for pride. It is not in any spirit of apology for our own past that we should approach this great problem. Rather should we approach it with abundant faith in ourselves, in the principles for which we stand, in the vision of a commonwealth of free nations transcending all differences of race or creed, and linking together East and West in the common cause of human progress. It is to those same principles, to that same vision, that we hope by sincerity, by good will, by patience if need be, to win the free and unfettered allegiance of our Indian fellow citizens. For the moment, if I may quote words used in this House by Burke of the difficulties of the Indian situation in his day:

> 'There we are....and we must do the best we can in our situation. The situation of man is the preceptor of his duty.'

XII

THE BRITISH COMMONWEALTH AND THE WORLD

THE OXFORD UNION, MARCH 6TH, 1942

This is no time for discussing in detail our war aims. We shall have to pass through many deep waters before the end is in sight, and, meanwhile, all our effort will need to be concentrated on the task of winning through. All the same it may be worth while pausing for a moment to ask ourselves certain very broad questions. What are we fighting for? What is it that we are up against? What shall we continue to be up against when the immediate issue of this war is settled?

We are fighting, in general terms, for freedom, for the freedom of nations, great and small, to live their own lives secure against aggression; freedom within the nations of thought and speech and political action; freedom from racial intolerance and persecution. On this more general issue we stand side by side with a host of freedom-loving peoples. But we are also fighting in a more intimate and passionate sense for our own existence, for freedom as embodied in the way of life and traditions of this little island and of the world-wide commonwealth which has sprung from its loins, and which, both in its individual members and in its collective stucture, is but an enlargement of the freedom we prize at home. Our freedom here is no mere abstraction, no mere mechanical device for collecting the votes of an arithmetical majority. It is a living organic thing, a tradition, an instinct, a heritage which has grown through the centuries. Its foundation was laid long centuries ago, in Norman law and order, order effective to protect freedom, but order —as Magna Charta insisted—under the law. On this foundation of the reign of law we have built up the superstructure of a system of free government based on the essential principle that the law of the land, which governments must obey, can only be changed and developed with the assent of the people. These fundamental principles we have carried with us wherever we have gone. Wherever conditions have allowed it our settlers have carried with them the whole system of freedom, both foundation and superstructure. Elsewhere, dealing with different conditions, where the tradition of free self-government was absent, we have at any rate laid the foundation of the reign of law, and have always kept in view the further stage of representative and responsible self-government.

You may have noticed that for the title of this address I have chosen the word 'Commonwealth'. I have done so advisedly, not because I am ashamed of the fine old word 'Empire', but because the term 'Commonwealth' —technically speaking confined to the self-governing parts of the Empire in their co-operative aspect—expresses our spirit and intention with regard to the future character of the whole. I have also done so for the particular reason that the term 'commonwealth' not only denotes the spirit of our association, but has also come to denote the peculiar structure of that association. Elsewhere kindred independent units have come together by the process of federation. They have divested themselves of certain defined elements of their sovereignty and transferred them to a new central authority. The system is one which has great merits, and is comparatively easy where the different units are geographically contiguous. But it creates many difficult problems and is not easily applicable where the units have a very different geographical or economic position or a strong national consciousness. It is worth noting that neither Newfoundland nor New Zealand ever took the opportunity open to them to join the Canadian or Australian federal systems. Many of us in my youth were ardent advocates of some system of Imperial federation. In fact, we have developed on a very different line. We have grown up to find ourselves a group of nations, united by allegiance to a common

Crown, the symbolic embodiment of our underlying unity of ideas and traditions, but working in a completely free and informal partnership over the whole field of national life. The British Commonwealth is, in fact, a free association of free nations for all purposes of their common security or common well being. Whether such an experiment can succeed, whether a political system so completely devoid of any rigid constitutional framework can, in the long run, stand either the strain of war or the centrifugal tendencies of peace, remains to be seen. We may well say today, paraphrasing the words of Abraham Lincoln, that we are engaged in a great war testing whether this commonwealth, or any commonwealth so conceived and dedicated, can long endure.

What then is it that this commonwealth is up against today? We are up against aggression and the lust of power run mad, against brutality, treachery, the denial of all the ideals which underlie our Christian civilization, or, indeed, any civilization which has a moral or religious basis. But that is not the whole story. If it were only moral depravity we were fighting, the struggle might be easier to dispose of. What we must realize is that we are up against a world revolution, a revolution acting with peculiarly eruptive and destructive force through particular centres of disturbance and intensifying particular national ambitions, but yet in itself a world-wide and continuing phenomenon. We are indeed confronted, not so much by a single revolution as by a double one, by a political revolution and by a technical revolution. The political revolution, like most other revolutions, is the outcome of the ideas of the study or the pulpit translating themselves, after a certain time-lag, into political thought and action and accompanied in the process, as is no less usual, by every kind of perversion, excess and internal and international conflict. To explain what I mean I need only ask you to cast your minds back for a moment to the French Revolution of 150 years ago, which translated into popular terms and raised to a plane of passionate emotion and action the rationalist, individualist theories of the great French thinkers and writers of the preceding generation. When the fury of the revolutionary wars was spent, the underlying ideas of that revolution became the foundation of the respectable Liberalism of the last century. Meanwhile the intellectual reaction against rationalist individualism, the reaction embodied in the philosophy of Hegel, in the growth of the conception of evolution in history as well as in biology, has laid increasing emphasis on the organic nature of human society and laid increasing stress upon the dominance of tradition and instinct, the importance of institutions and symbols, the ineffectiveness of mere abstract reason, in human affairs. In violent reaction against the weakness and incoherence of Liberal and Socialist democracies on the Continent it has crystallized into the extravagance of the Totalitarian State. In reaction against pacifist idealism it has asserted the law of the survival of the fittest in its crudest form—the law of the jungle. Blended with the Prussian militarist tradition, with fantastic racial theories and ambitions, with a desire to be revenged for past defeat and humiliation, and, not least, with the despair of mass unemployment, it produced the German Revolution, with its Robespierre and Napoleon rolled into one in the fantastic figure of Adolf Hitler.

Simultaneously we are passing through a tremendous technical revolution. The French Revolution took place under conditions of production and communications which, save for the mariner's compass and the discovery of America, had hardly changed since the days of the Antonines. The industrial revolution which followed and the opening up of the resources of the world by steamship and the railway, saw revolutionary frenzy settled down into the bourgeois capitalism of the second half of the last century. The new technical revolution with its mass production on a gigantic scale, but more particularly with the two new factors of aviation and the wireless and its power of mass propaganda, have enormously intensified not only the economic and consequently fighting potential of the organized State, but also its organized and drilled will-power. It is that new phenomenon, the highly organized State, planned and directed, yet at the same time inspired by a terrific unity and concentration of purpose, that we are fighting today.

We, here, meanwhile have been carrying on, in our social and political structure, on the basis of nineteenth-century *laisser faire*, and are today painfully struggling to improvise our war organization and to turn ourselves into the kind of engine of power into which countries like Germany, Japan, and Russia turned themselves years ago. If that is true of this country itself, it is even more true of other parts of the British Commonwealth and of that Commonwealth regarded as a whole. Our Commonwealth is essentially one that has grown up by the methods of *laisser faire* and individual enterprise behind the shield of sea-power won at Trafalgar. We have never seriously contemplated the possibility of that sea-power being weakened, even temporarily or locally, or of individual members of the Commonwealth being so organized as to be capable of defending themselves against a powerful adversary. Within striking distance, under modern conditions, of Japan, Australia has grown up, not on any planned policy of developing its resources for defence or economic production to match possible dangers, but to such extent as individual capitalists or immigrants have happened to be attracted by its opportunities, or their inflow restricted by its legislation. What is true of the Dominions has been even more true of that dependent Empire for which we here have been responsible. We have looked after it according to the best of our lights within the limits of our political outlook; and within the limits of that outlook we have no reason to be ashamed of our handiwork.

It has suddenly become the fashion after our recent defeats to decry the British Colonial system, more particularly in the Far East. Let me remind you of what, after all, it achieved and what it stood for. Let me take Hong Kong and Singapore. There, a century ago, Britain acquired a barren rock inhabited by a handful of fishermen, and a derelict village in a mangrove swamp.

British administration, British justice and fair play, drew to those two spots the enterprise and capital of all the world, as well as of this country, and an eager concourse of willing workers from neighbouring countries. They made of them two of the world's most prosperous and happy communities. In Malaya British protection put an end to piracy and the internecine quarrels of minor States. Without interfering with the traditions, the loyalties and way of life of the Malay population, it found opportunities for the creative enterprise of Europeans and the free and effective co-operation of other immigrant communities, Chinese and Indian. All of these lived happily together in a little cosmopolitan world free both from racial oppression and racial bitterness. The one thing we did not do was to prepare them for war. We neither enforced military training on them nor taxed them (beyond a trifling local contribution in the case of Singapore, and generous voluntary contributions from the Malay rulers), for their own defence or the common defence of the Empire. We were proud of that policy. Today we may realize its inadequacy to meet the dangers we should perhaps have foreseen. But it ill becomes those who, in the past, were most vocal in denouncing the British Empire as an empire of militarism and oppression, now to turn round and complain because the peoples of Malaya were unarmed, untrained and, above all, unused to the thought of war. It is equally absurd to suggest that some wider measure of local self-government would have made any material difference in that respect. The example of Siam next door, or of Denmark at the other end of the world, show well enough that independence by itself offers no guarantee of the power of resistance of a people who have never learnt, or have forgotten, to take heed to their defence.

The same is in no small measure true of India. It has been our boast that India was never deliberately conquered by British arms, that our empire in India grew aided only by a handful of mainly local troops, and that it grew and maintained itself for the simple reason that it was acceptable to the people of India. We were proud that a mere handful, again mainly of Indian troops, preserved the peace of that empire. At the outbreak of war the army in India numbered some 230,000 men, one soldier to every 1,500 of the population of India ; one British soldier to every 6,000 of the population. Even so the main complaint of political India has always been the inordinate scale and expense of India's military organization. Even we ourselves have felt misgivings on the score that we were asking too much of a poor country, and when, shortly before the war, it came to the question of even a partial mechanization of the Indian Army, we felt it our duty to contribute towards the expense. When the war began we had practically no war equipment ourselves here, nor even enough of the equipment with which to begin making the equipment of war. It was at no small sacrifice that even a portion of our slowly growing supply of munitions, and of the machine tools and skilled personnel with which to make munitions, could be spared to contribute to help India's military expansion. Compared with the slenderness of its original resources and the inevitable difficulty of access to the means of production the Government of India has achieved wonders in the expansion, training, and equipment of its armies. Nothing surely could be more inconsistent than that the people who, a few years ago, denounced the militarism of the Government of India and the crushing burdens imposed on a poor country by the exiguous pre-war preparations, should now suggest that millions of armed and trained warriors could be stamped out of the ground overnight by some political declaration.

We shall win through somehow. But that will not be the end of the story. We shall defeat the German and the Japanese fury as we defeated the fury of revolutionary France and the military genius of Napoleon. But the new world forces which are being liberated today will not cease working. The genie cannot be imprisoned in his bottle again. The forces of which I speak are economic as well as military, or rather the same forces can find their expression equally in military or economic power—in guns or butter, to quote Goering. It seems to me obvious that in the world of the future the organized community and State, or group of States, must displace, whether in peace or in war, the unorganized, just as, for most purposes, machine production has displaced hand production. By that I do not mean, of course, that the world of the future is to be handed over to totalitarian or servile regimes. On the contrary, I believe that the most effective and enduring of all forms of organization will be that which free men work out for themselves.

The problem, moreover, is one not merely of structure but of size. Every factor in the technical development of the world today is in favour of the larger unit. We have already seen something of the helplessness of the small State whose principal cities can be blotted out in half an hour by the overwhelming air force of a powerful neighbour. In the economic field, too, modern mass production demands for its efficiency and stability both a large home market and the control of a wide range of resources. The larger indeed the unit the less the strain upon its structure and the greater the room for freedom of individual action within it. It is the immense size and immense resources of the United States, insulated, both geographically and economically, from the outside world, that have enabled its internal structure to retain its so essentially individualist character.

In any case it seems to me that the inevitable tendency of the post-war world will be towards the agglomeration of political communities otherwise inadequate in dimensions and resources to sustain any true independence. One way of achieving this result is that of conquest and domination—the way of Hitler's New Order, the way of Japan's Far Eastern 'co-prosperity sphere'. The other is by free and equal co-operation. Must that co-operation necessarily follow the rigid path of federalism ? Or can it be based on the more flexible principle of the commonwealth ? In other words, do I believe that the British Commonwealth, if it survives this war, as I am certain it will, is capable of surviving the stress of the subsequent generation ?

I believe that it can so survive, but only on certain conditions. The first is that each part must individually organize its own life far more effectively. We here shall have to recast our social and economic life in many directions. I believe we can do so without loss of individual freedom or of personality, without injury to the essential character of our national life and with benefit to every class in the community. The same is true of each of the Dominions. It is, above all, true perhaps of India, whose future problem is even more a question of raising the general standard of life and of creating that surplus above bare existence which means both welfare and power. Nutrition, industrial development, improvement of agricultural methods, education, these are perhaps the most important of all issues that will face India after the war, whatever her form of government. But, secondly, if we are to survive individually and also to do so on the basis of the greatest possible measure of individual freedom, then we must work together more closely than we have before in our system of free union. We must perfect the machinery of common consultation, of co-operation in defence and in trade, in the mutually planned development of our population and resources. On these conditions I believe our Commonwealth can not only survive, but prosper beyond the boldest imagination of any of us, and by so doing give an example of infinite value to the rest of the world.

I know there is a school of thought who would have us abandon the commonwealth experiment in favour of some form of federal union with the United States and possibly with certain other democratic communities. I do not believe myself that such a union is feasible even among Anglo-Saxon communities. Our traditions, though kindred, have diverged too far in the last 160 years. In any case such a federal union, if it included Britain and the Dominions of European origin, could hardly include India or our Colonial Empire. That, in other words, would mean the end of an empire or commonwealth based, not on race, but on institutions and ideals, and would open out a dangerous vista of future world racial conflicts. We are all naturally and rightly in favour of the most intimate co-operation after this war with the United States for our common welfare and for the peace of the world, but I believe that will be best achieved, not by absorption into some rigid federal scheme, but by free and equal co-operation, in which the British Commonwealth can serve not only as a bridge and interpreter between America and Europe, but also between the Western world and Asia, and so help to prefigure and pave the way towards the future commonwealth of mankind.

If we are to fulfil this high task it is essential that we should have faith in ourselves, in our ideals and in our methods. It is the fashion today to run down the imperialism of an earlier generation, the imperialism of Rhodes and Chamberlain and Kipling. That imperialism may sometimes have struck a narrow, arrogant, and even blatant note. But it had faith in itself and in the good it was doing and was destined to do to the peoples with whom it dealt and to the world. The strength of that faith and the seriousness of its idealism were perhaps best expressed in that great statesman, Lord Milner, and explained the profound influence which he exercised upon so many of the younger men who came in contact with him. The tragedy of the inter-war years was the loss in faith in anything living and concrete, a faith for which enthusiasm about abstract phrases and vague schemes involving no effort or sacrifice can never be a sufficient substitute. The world has changed much in the fifty years since I first attended a debate in this House. It has been changing at an ever-accelerating rate. It will change even more rapidly in the future. It is for you here to shape that future. It has been said that faith can move mountains. Your faith, if only you have faith, can assuredly shape the future both of the British Commonwealth and of the world as your vision and your ideals will bid you shape it.

APPENDIX I

STATEMENT ISSUED WITH THE AUTHORITY OF HIS MAJESTY'S GOVERNMENT BY THE GOVERNOR-GENERAL ON AUGUST 8TH, 1940

INDIA's anxiety at this moment of critical importance in the world struggle against tyranny and aggression to contribute to the full to the common cause and to the triumph of our common ideals is manifest. She has already made a mighty contribution. She is anxious to make a greater contribution still. His Majesty's Government are deeply concerned that that unity of national purpose in India which would enable her to do so should be achieved at as early a moment as possible. They feel that some further statement of their intentions may help to promote that unity. In that hope they have authorized me to make the present statement.

Last October His Majesty's Government again made it clear that Dominion Status was their objective for India. They added that they were ready to authorize the expansion of the Governor-General's Council to include a certain number of representatives of the political parties, and they proposed the establishment of a consultative committee. In order to facilitate harmonious co-operation, it was obvious that some measure of agreement in the Provinces between the major parties was a desirable prerequisite to their joint collaboration at the Centre. Such agreement was, unfortunately, not reached, and in the circumstances no progress was then possible.

During the earlier part of this year I continued my efforts to bring the political parties together. In these last few weeks I again entered into conversations with prominent political personages in British India and the Chancellor of the Chamber of Princes, the results of which have been reported to His Majesty's Government. His Majesty's Government have seen also the resolutions passed by the Congress Working Committee, the Moslem League and the Hindu Mahasabha.

It is clear that earlier differences which had prevented the achievement of national unity remain unbridged. Deeply as His Majesty's Government regret this, they do not feel that they should any longer, because of those differences, postpone the expansion of the Governor-General's Council, and the establishment of a body which will more closely associate Indian public opinion with the conduct of the war by the Central Government. They have authorized me accordingly to invite a certain number of representative Indians to join my Executive Council. They have authorized me further to establish a War Advisory Council which would contain representatives of the Indian States and of other interests in the national life of India as a whole.

The conversations which have taken place, and the resolutions of the bodies which I have just mentioned, made it clear, however, that there is still in certain quarters doubt as to the intentions of His Majesty's Government for the constitutional future of India, and that there is doubt, too, as to whether the position of minorities, whether political or religious, is sufficiently safeguarded in relation to any future constitutional change by assurances already given. There are two main points that have emerged. On those two points His Majesty's Government now desire me to make their position clear.

The first is as to the position of minorities in relation to any future constitutional scheme. It has already been made clear that my declaration of last October does not exclude examination of any part either of the Act of 1935 or of the policy and plans on which it is based. His Majesty's Government's concern that full weight should be given to the views of minorities in any revision has also been brought out. That remains the position of His Majesty's Government.

It goes without saying that they could not contemplate transfer of their present responsibilities for the peace and welfare of India to any system of government whose authority is directly denied by large and powerful elements in India's national life. Nor could they be parties to the coercion of such elements into submission to such a Government.

The second point of general interest is the machinery for building within the British Commonwealth of Nations the new constitutional scheme when the time comes. There has been very strong insistence that the framing of that scheme should be primarily the responsibility of Indians themselves, and should originate from Indian conceptions of the social, economic and political structure of Indian life. His Majesty's Government are in sympathy with that desire and wish to see it given the fullest practical expression, subject to the due fulfilment of the obligations which Great Britain's long connexion with India has imposed on her and for which His Majesty's Government cannot divest themselves of responsibility. It is clear that a moment when the Commonwealth is engaged in a struggle for existence is not one in which fundamental constitutional issues can be decisively resolved. But His Majesty's Government authorize me to declare that they will most readily assent to the setting up after the conclusion of the war with the least possible delay of a body representative of the principal elements in India's national life in order to devise the framework of the new Constitution, and they will lend every aid in their power to hasten decisions on all relevant matters to the utmost degree. Meanwhile they will welcome and promote in any way possible every sincere and practical step that may be taken by representative Indians themselves to reach a basis of friendly agreement, first upon the form which the post-war representative body should take and the methods by which it should arrive at its conclusions, and secondly, upon the principles and outlines of the Constitution itself. They trust, however, that for the period of the war (with the Central Government reconstituted and strengthened in the manner I have described, and with the help of the War Advisory Council) all parties, communities and interests will combine and co-operate in making a notable Indian contribution to the victory of the world cause which is at stake. Moreover, they hope that in this process new bonds of union and understanding will emerge, and thus pave the way towards the attainment by India of that free and equal partnership in the British Commonwealth which remains the proclaimed and accepted goal of the Imperial Crown and of the British Parliament.

APPENDIX II

DRAFT DECLARATION FOR DISCUSSION WITH INDIAN LEADERS AS PUBLISHED ON MARCH 30TH, 1942

(The conclusions of the British War Cabinet set out below were those which Sir Stafford Cripps took with him for discussion with the Indian leaders. In view of the disagreement, on various and contradictory grounds, of the different parties with the proposals concerning the future, as well as of the demands of the Congress Party for the immediate transfer of the Government of India to an Indian 'National Government', the declaration was never issued as such.)

HIS MAJESTY'S GOVERNMENT having considered the anxieties expressed in this country and in India as to the fulfilment of the promises made in regard to the future of India, have decided to lay down in precise and clear terms the steps which they propose shall be taken for the earliest possible realization of self-government in India. The object is the creation of a new Indian Union which shall constitute a Dominion, associated with the United Kingdom, and the other Dominions, by a common allegiance to the Crown, but equal to them in every respect, in no way subordinate in any respect of its domestic or external affairs.

His Majesty's Government therefore make the following declaration:

(*a*) Immediately upon the cessation of hostilities, steps shall be taken to set up in India, in the manner described hereafter, an elected body charged with the task of framing a new Constitution for India.

(*b*) Provision shall be made, as set out below, for the participation of the Indian States in the Constitution-making body.

(*c*) His Majesty's Government undertake to accept and implement forthwith the Constitution so framed subject only to:

(i) the right of any Province of British India that is not prepared to accept the new Constitution to retain its present constitutional position, provision being made for its subsequent accession if it so decides.

With such non-acceding Provinces, should they so desire, His Majesty's Government will be prepared to agree upon a new Constitution giving them the same full status as the Indian Union and arrived at by a procedure analogous to that here laid down.

(ii) the signing of a Treaty which shall be negotiated between His Majesty's Government and the Constitution-making body. This Treaty will cover all necessary matters arising out of the complete transfer of responsibility from British to Indian hands; it will make provision, in accordance with the undertakings given by His Majesty's Government, for the protection of racial and religious minorities: but will not impose any restriction on the power of the Indian Union to decide in the future its relationship to the other Member States of the British Commonwealth.

Whether or not an Indian State elects to adhere to the Constitution, it will be necessary to negotiate a revision of its Treaty arrangements, so far as this may be required in the new situation.

(*d*) The Constitution-making body shall be composed as follows, unless the leaders of Indian opinion in the principal communities agree upon some other form before the end of hostilities:

Immediately upon the result being known of the Provincial Elections which will be necessary at the end of hostilities, the entire membership of the Lower Houses of the Provincial Legislatures shall, as a single electoral college, proceed to the election of the Constitution-making body by the system of proportional representation. This new body shall be in number about one-tenth of the number of the electoral college.

Indian States shall be invited to appoint representatives in the same proportion to their total population as in the case of representatives of British India as a whole, and with the same powers as the British Indian members.

(*e*) During the critical period which now faces India and until the new Constitution can be framed His Majesty's Government must inevitably bear the responsibility for and retain the control and direction of the defence of India as part of their World War effort, but the task of organizing to the full the military, moral and material resources of India must be the responsibility of the Government of India with the co-operation of the peoples of India. His Majesty's Government desire and invite the immediate and effective participation of the leaders of the principal sections of the Indian people in the counsels of their country, of the Commonwealth and of the United Nations. Thus they will be enabled to give their active and constructive help in the discharge of a task which is vital and essential for the future freedom of India.